Foyle's Hastings

Large print or audio version available on request. Call 01424 451772

Produced, designed and published by Hastings Borough Council - Reprinted March 2006
Printed in Hastings by Hastings Printing Company Ltd, on paper from sustainable sources.
Photographs by Bob Mazzer, Chris Parker and Hastings Observer.

ISBN 0-901536-07-5

Welcome to Foyle's Hastings

This is your unofficial guide to the many Hastings & St Leonards locations made famous by the popular ITV detective show.

The show has proved incredibly popular both at home and abroad, with many fans being inspired to visit the town.

Use this guide to discover the special relationship that can sometimes exist between the reality of a place and the fiction of a television programme.

Contents:

THINK BEFORE YOU ACT. BUT THINK ALWAYS OF YOUR COUNTRY BEFORE YOU THINK OF YOURSELF.

Background

Initial filming for the Foyle's War pilot episode took place in Summer 2001 and in April 2002, filming for the first series began in earnest. Production company Greenlit Productions moved into the Old Town and took over Hill Street, Swan Terrace, Croft Road and High Street. The first series was broadcast in November that year to rave reviews. Viewers were won over by the series' low-key, gentle mystery and its unique period charm. Hastings & St Leonards residents took pleasure in spotting familiar locations and the way in which their geography was often rewritten in the editing process. Since then, Foyle's War and Hastings have become affectionately linked. Production crews have returned to the town to film for series two, three and four. Locations outside of the town have also been used, but the illusion of the stories being completely based in Hastings is never spoiled. The maritime charm and intimate atmosphere of the town is always maintained, despite some dramatic and often dark storylines.

The show was created by acclaimed author Anthony Horowitz who is also responsible for Midsomer Murders and the popular Alex Rider children's books. Although other South Coast location have been renamed, Horowitz made the decision to let Hastings keep its name in the show after learning that the town had a 'unique position' in World War II. So alongside its world-famous reputation as the birthplace of television and the site of the 1066 battle, Hastings has also become known as the home of Detective Chief Superintendent (DCS) Foyle. Anthony Horowitz seems delighted with the reception he and the crew receive in Hastings & St Leonards, he said: "Shooting here is a joy — we love being here."

The show follows the life of DCS Foyle, a police officer kept out of the war effort by injury. He dedicates his time to solving crimes at home in the South East of England. With viewing figures around 9 million per episode in the UK and an estimated worldwide fan base of over 60 million, the popularity of Foyle's War is indisputable.

Anthony Horowitz

FOYLES WAR II

SLATE 1477   TAKE 1

PANAVISION

DIR: JEREMY SILBERSTON
CAM: ALAN ALMOND   BSC

1ST AUGUST 2003 A

RX59

Filming

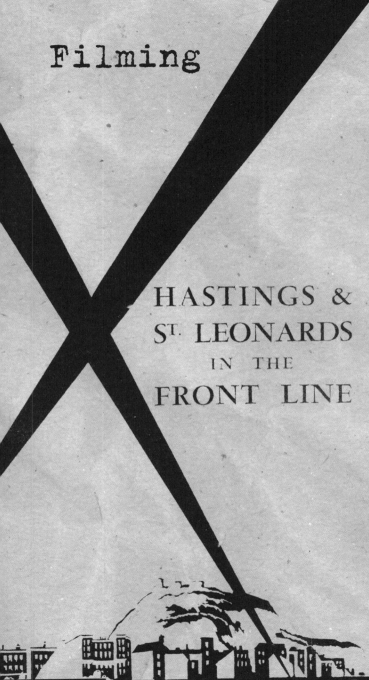

HASTINGS & ST. LEONARDS IN THE FRONT LINE

The logistics of filming in Hastings are at times a little complex. Access to roads needs to be restricted without causing too much disruption for motorists, shoots on the busy fishing beach need to be organised and the cast and crew need somewhere to stay. Hastings residents take pride in welcoming the cast and crew to their town, making the job a little easier. The cast and production crew all stay locally in various hotels, and the local council is always accommodating, providing support, advice and even parking attendants!

There is quite an art to achieving 1940s authenticity in Hastings & St Leonards. The Old Town may not have as many modern give-aways as elsewhere but there is still a lot of work to do to conceal evidence of the modern world. All 21st century vehicles, road signs and markings, road coverings and street furniture have to be hidden. In addition aerials, satellite dishes and burglar alarms all have to be dealt with. Even hanging baskets are removed and replaced with flower boxes. Fake greenery hides chicken wire, patio doors or illuminated street signs. Victorian style hollow lamppost covers, like drainpipes are fitted over modern streetlights and period covers are fitted to bollards. Also, street lines and markings are covered with gravel. Period cars such as butcher's vans or removal vans are used to hide things in the street that can't be moved, and newspaper stands cover up other modern day give-aways. Modern double glazed windows present a problem for the production crew, who sometimes board up houses (a wartime bomb blast defence) so windows can be concealed.

12

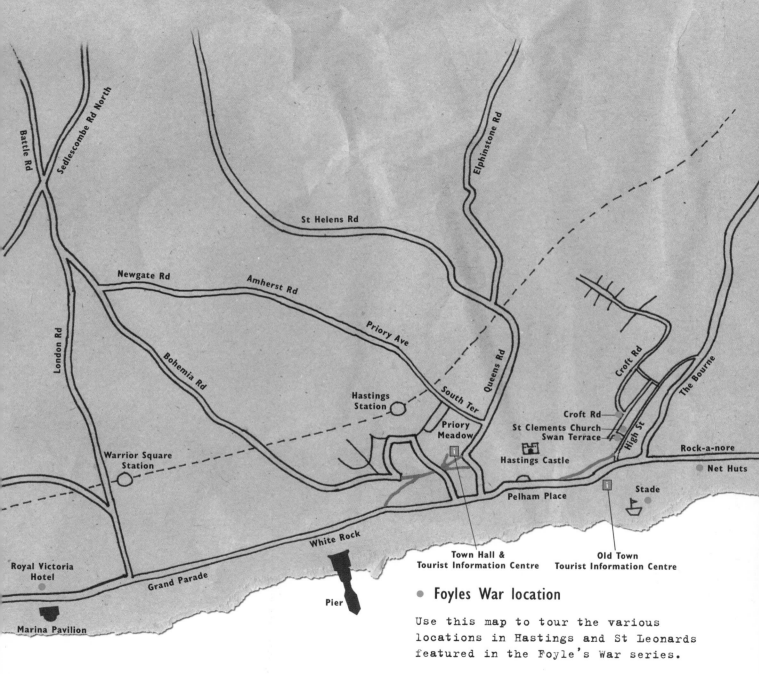

Battle Rd

Sedlescombe Rd North

St Helens Rd

Elphinstone Rd

Newgate Rd

Amherst Rd

Priory Ave

London Rd

Bohemia Rd

Queens Rd

Croft Rd

The Bourne

Hastings
Station

South Ter

Croft Rd

St Clements Church
Swan Terrace

High St

Rock-a-nore

Warrior Square
Station

Priory
Meadow

Hastings Castle

Net Huts

Stade

Pelham Place

White Rock

Town Hall &
Tourist Information Centre

Old Town
Tourist Information Centre

Royal Victoria
Hotel

Grand Parade

Pier

● Foyles War location

Use this map to tour the various
locations in Hastings and St Leonards
featured in the Foyle's War series.

Marina Pavilion

14

Locations

Swan Terrace

This small terrace runs next to St Clements Church off High Street. The church appears every time Honeysuckle Weeks' character, Sam, drives up to the house where DCS Foyle lives in the show. The church was also used in a scene where DCS Foyle and Sam are together on the National Day of Prayer.

At the bottom of Swan Terrace is a memorial garden where The Swan Inn once stood before it was destroyed in an enemy air raid during World War Two.

In one episode of the show, DCS Foyle drives down Swan Terrace past the memorial gardens. Although the episode is set in 1940, the Swan Inn was not destroyed until three years later. In reality in 1940, Christopher Foyle would have passed a very different scene at the bottom of Swan Terrace to that which can be seen today.

Croft Road

The house on the corner of Croft Road is where the show's lead character Detective Chief Superintendent Christopher Foyle lives. In the show the road is known as Steep Street. The house itself is quite striking, and is arguably one of the most memorable buildings used in the show. Croft Road is a busy, but narrow residential street in the Old Town. Access to the road has to be restricted during filming, causing a little disruption to residents. Typically welcoming, the Old Town folk are always willing to put up with the restrictions to help the crew.

Croft Road is a short walk off the High Street by the side of St Clements Church; follow the road round to the right and up the hill. Foyle's house is number 31 on the left hand side. Any fan of the show will instantly recognise the unusual façade.

Other locations in the Old Town are also featured in the show, such as Hill Street and Post Office Passage. Why not take a walk through the Old Town and see how many of the streets and buildings seem familiar?

The Stade

This steep shingle beach is home to Europe's largest beach-launched fishing fleet and was used extensively in the series one episode 'The White Feather'.

The beach has been known as The Stade for over a thousand years, the name comes from a Saxon word meaning 'landing place'. The steep gradient of the beach means that the fishing boats can slide into the sea at high tide but they have to be hauled out on their return. This prevents them from being more than ten metres long so they can only carry small amounts of gear over short distances.

The Net Huts

These historic buildings were another element of Hastings fishing heritage used. They featured heavily in the episode 'The German Woman' during a tense chase sequence. The net huts, or net shops, as they are also known locally, are distinct landmarks unique to Hastings. Fishermen used these tall shed-like buildings to store their nets.

The weatherboarded and tarred structures date from the 19th century. At this time, space was at a premium, but fishermen needed space to store their nets, otherwise they'd rot - so they built upwards! Restored with a Heritage Lottery Grant, they're now one of the town's most important landmarks.

The Royal Victoria Hotel

This is one of the town's most historic and striking buildings. It was used by the Foyle's War crew in the episode 'Eagle Day' when Detective Chief Superintendent Foyle and Detective Sergeant Milner are called to investigate a stabbed body found in the aftermath of a bombing raid. During the filming for this episode, the A259 outside the hotel, one of the UK's busiest roads, had to be temporarily closed!

Originally known as the St Leonards Hotel it was renamed after Queen Victoria's patronage. Her signature can still be seen in the Visitors' Book.

The hotel was built by James Burton who lived from 1761 to 1837 and was probably one of the most significant builders of Georgian London. In 1828 he started building a new seaside town at St Leonards, based closely on his ideas and experiences at Regents Park.

The Royal Victoria Hotel is located on the A259 at St Leonards.

Victoria

The Pier

Rubber barbed wire was set up on the beach for a scene beneath the Pier in an early episode. As with most piers, Hastings was sectioned during the Second World War for fear of German invasion, cutting off the main pier structure from the shore promenade. Although suffering some bomb damage, the Pier was reopened in 1946.

First opened in 1872, the Pier was once home to three halls, the Pier Pavilion, the Pier Theatre and a bandstand. Following a recent refurbishment the Pier is looking refreshed and renewed. It has become a popular attraction thanks to the distinctive range of shops, restaurants and entertainment venues it houses.

The Pier had a particularly lively role during the 1920s and 30s. During this period Hastings Pier provided much entertainment. There was dancing every night, daytime concerts, stunt diving, and speedboat trips out to the harbour and back. A searchlight was even fitted to the Pier to provide adequate light for the youngsters who dared to go midnight swimming.

Hastings Pier is located towards the St Leonards end of the seafront, in the direction of Bexhill on the A259.

Locals get involved

Hastings fishermen were used as extras to help in the recreation of the Dunkirk evacuation in series one. Local fisherman Graham Bossom's boat took the role of Lady Rose. Graham and fellow fishermen were caught up in the action, taking parts as extras. They physically launched and recovered a fishing boat using old fashioned methods, and also played parts as wounded soldiers. The episode's portrayal of the Dunkirk evacuation was partly fiction; no Hastings fishing boats took part but the Hastings lifeboat did. This dramatic event was re-enacted on Hastings beach, bringing home the disturbing horror of the Dunkirk evacuation.

What will happen to me if I don't stay put?

If you do not stay put you will stand a very good chance of being killed. The enemy may machine-gun you from the air in order to increase panic, or you may run into enemy forces which have landed behind you.

Hastings at War

Here we explore a little of the reality of wartime Hastings.

Hastings was often bombed during the Second World War. The Old Town and areas of the town centre both suffered badly from enemy attacks. In total, there were 85 enemy air attacks on the town. The first came on July 26 1940 and the last on August 2 1944.

In the first attack, a single aircraft dropped 11 bombs, several of which fell on the cricket ground. After these attacks however, it was claimed by German bombers that several successful hits had been made on Hastings harbour. Not quite the reality of what happened on the ground.

September 1940 saw a quite disastrous attack on Hastings town centre. Significant damage was caused to Queens Road, Nelson Road, Milward Road and St Mary's Terrace. On September 30, a bomb hit the front of the Plaza cinema in Robertson Street where Yates' Wine Lodge now stands. Eight people were killed instantly in this incident with four others dying later from their injuries. Significant damage was caused to the memorial area in general. The four dials of the memorial clock were blown out and many shops in the area sustained serious damage.

Possibly the worst attack on Hastings during the war came in March 1943, when around 30 aircraft dropped 25 powerful bombs randomly across the town. The attack caused shocking devastation. In this raid, 38 people lost their lives, 39 were seriously injured and 51 sustained minor injuries. The Silverhill area of the town suffered particularly badly, many buildings were irreparably damaged. Houses in Battle Road, Bury Road, Perth Road and Sedlescombe Road North suffered serious damage, and in Adelaide Road several homes were wrecked.

In total during WWII, 550 High Explosive Bombs, 12 Oil Incendiary Bombs, 750 Small Incendiary Bombs and 15 V1 flying bombs were dropped on the town. There were 154 recorded deaths, 260 people injured needing hospital treatment and 439 were slightly injured as a result of enemy air attacks. A total of 436 houses were demolished either by direct hit or as a result of damage sustained in attacks.

and Now—

HASTINGS
AND
ST. LEONARDS
are getting ready for your
Invasion

Parsons, Ltd., London and Hastings

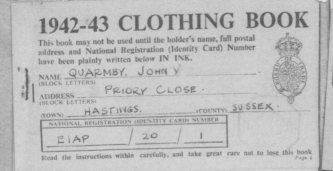

1942-43 CLOTHING BOOK

This book may not be used until the holder's name, full postal address and National Registration (Identity Card) Number have been plainly written below IN INK.

NAME QUARMBY. JOHN V
(BLOCK LETTERS)
ADDRESS PRIORY CLOSE.
(BLOCK LETTERS)
(TOWN) HASTINGS. (COUNTY) SUSSEX.

NATIONAL REGISTRATION (IDENTITY CARD) NUMBER

| EIAP | 20 | 1 |

Read the instructions within carefully, and take great care not to lose this book *Page 4*

MINISTRY OF FOOD. Serial No. T 23 Nº 007548
TRAVELLER'S RATION BOOK.

INSTRUCTIONS. [Read carefully.]

N.11.
Continued on back cover.

31

SMUGGLERS ADVENTURE

21 STOCKLEIGH
ST. LEONARDS

The Old Town

The beginning of war brought about change in the Old Town. Redevelopment came to a halt and large areas were left empty. Barbed wire, gun emplacements and tank traps were seen along the seafront. No access was allowed to the beach during wartime. Fishermen were allowed exceptional access to continue working. They took a great risk going to sea at this time - three boats were lost in mine explosions.

A number of people took refuge in St. Clements caves, which were used as an air raid shelter, hospital and school and were known to have housed 300 to 400 people. The caves are now home to the popular Smugglers Adventure.

As a result of the numerous bombing raids and possibility of German landings in the area, many residents were evacuated. By 1940 the town's population had been reduced by about two thirds.

34

Ministry of Information in co-operation with the War Office and the Ministry of Home Security.

The Old Town suffered its worst attack on May 23 1943 when the Swan Inn in the High Street was destroyed. It was a busy Sunday lunchtime when sixteen people were killed in the attack which also destroyed numbers 1,2 and 3 Swan Terrace. A plaque now commemorates where the inn once stood, it reads:

On this site stood THE SWAN INN & 1,2 & 3 SWAN TERRACE destroyed by enemy action at about mid-day on Sunday 23 May 1943 with consider-able loss of life.

OLD TOWN HALL MUSEUM

you should obey the second rule, which is as follows:—

(2) DO NOT BELIEVE RUMOURS AND DO NOT SPREAD THEM. WHEN YOU RECEIVE AN ORDER, MAKE QUITE SURE THAT IT IS A TRUE ORDER AND NOT A FAKED ORDER. MOST OF YOU KNOW YOUR POLICEMEN AND YOUR A.R.P. WARDENS BY SIGHT, YOU CAN TRUST THEM. IF YOU KEEP YOUR HEADS, YOU CAN ALSO TELL WHETHER A MILITARY OFFICER IS REALLY BRITISH OR ONLY PRETENDING TO BE SO. IF IN DOUBT ASK THE POLICE-MAN OR THE A.R.P. WARDEN. USE YOUR COMMON SENSE.

35

MINISTRY OF FOOD

RATION BOOK

OFFICIAL PAID

HOLDER'S NAME AND REGISTERED ADDRESS

Compare with your Identity Card and report any difference to your Food Office

DO NOT ALTER

ISSUED
JULY 1942

If found return to

BATTLE

FOOD OFFICE

Surname CROFT

Other Names Ethel L.

Address The Beeches

Netherfield.

Battle

S.x

NAT. REG. No.	EKBN	38	3

SERIAL NUMBER OF BOOK

RG 432392

R.B.1 General

NATIONAL REGISTRATION

IDENTITY CARD

IF FOUND
RETURN TO
ANY FOOD OFFICE

RATIONING SCHEME

Certain foods, soon after the outbreak of a war, would be brought under a rationing scheme similar to that which was introduced during the latter part of the Great War. In the first instance, rationing would be applied to five foodstuffs—butcher's meat, bacon and ham, sugar, butter and margarine, and cooking fats. Later, it might be necessary to add other articles.

The object of this scheme is to make certain that foodstuffs are distributed fairly and equally and that everyone is sure of his or her proper share.

HOW TO PATCH A SHIRT
by
Mrs. SEW-and-SEW

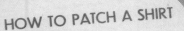

● Shirts are easy to mend, as the patches can be cut from other parts of the garment. They can be replaced by similar material cut from a discarded shirt, or soft cotton. When the cuffs start to fray, they should be carefully unpicked and reversed. As they are double, the worn edge will then be inside the fold. If you are using new fabric for patching, it should be washed first.

NYLON NEWS
FROM MRS. SEW-and-SEW
ISSUED BY THE BOARD OF TRADE

to look after Parachute Nylon

...lon appearing in the shops at the moment is ...ute nylon, so don't expect all the advantages ...ear's nylon will offer.

THIS IS HOW TO WASH NYLON

Use warm water and dissolve the soap thoroughly. Rinse repeatedly to remove all trace of suds. You may rub or wring the fabric, but it is not advisable to twist it. As nylon fabric dries very quickly, it is an advantage to iron it as soon as possible after washing.

In the case of coloured goods, be sure that the colours are fast. If they are inclined to run, wash the garment by it...lf.

...OW TO REINFORCE FOR
...TRA WEAR
...rs. SEW-and-SEW

...is strengthening a new garment at ...e you know the wear will be greatest. ...one on the wrong side and it should ...the right side if it is neatly sewn. ... for most work, but herringbone ...e used on woven fabrics and flannel. ...s are left raw. Tape or bias binding ... useful for strengthening seams.

...W TO PATCH SHEETS
AND BLANKETS
by
Mrs. Sew - and - Sew

● When choosing piece for patch, make sure the selvedge runs the same way as on the article to be patched. Patches on household linen should be edge-stitched by machine and the corners made square and very strong. If the area to be patched is very near the edge, make the patch large enough to reach the edge allowing sufficient material to make ...hem along the outer side, or round new corner.

MH 2843781   MH 2843781

Motor Fuel Ration Book

MOTOR CAR
1101 – 1500
C.C.

10 – 13.
H.P.

Registered No. of Vehicle   Registered No. of Vehicle

Date and Office of Issue

This book is the property of Her Majesty's Government

...Se... is ...th Rat... Book Recorded on the applicant's registration book.

This portion, after completion, to be detached and forwarded to the Regional Petroleum Officer with Form P.221B

The coupons in this book authori... ...ining and acquisition of the number of units of motor fuel specified in the coupons.

[handwritten note:] Great ... ...garde... mother and dad take care of yourself mother I love you

[table of ration coupons showing repeated: BACON, Marg., Ckg. Fats, Butter, SPARE ONE, with numbers 1–16, 35, 45, 32, 42, 21, 18, 17, 3, 7, 4, 31, etc.]

VIA AIR ...
...4...

Useful Information

For information about accommodation, local attractions and much more visit:

Hastings Information Centre
Priory Meadow
Queens Square
Hastings

Call 0845 274 1001

Log on to **www.visithastings.com** for more pictures of Foyle's War filming. And also for accommodation, events and entertainment listings.

Fans of Foyle's War may be interested in the range of WWII exhibits on show at:

Hastings Old Town Hall Museum
High Street
Hastings

Call 01424 781166

Additional Reading

The following publications are all available from Hastings Information Centre

Hastings at War
By Nathan Dylan Goodwin
Priced £12.99

Letters from Lavender Cottage: Hastings in WWII and Austerity
By Victoria Seymour
Priced £7.99

Hastings in Peace and War
By Mary Haskell Porter
Priced £7.50

The Weekend Cook

The Weekend Cook

JANET · HORSLEY

COLLINS
8 GRAFTON STREET, LONDON
1987

Dedication To Carol Martin

William Collins Sons & Co. Ltd.
London · Glasgow · Sydney · Auckland
Toronto · Johannesburg

First published 1987

© Janet Horsley 1987
© Illustrations by Katherine Greenwood 1987

Horsley, Janet
The Weekend Cook
1. Cookery, International
I. Title
641.5   TX725.A1
ISBN 0 00 411230 X

Filmset in Galliard by
V & M Graphics Ltd, Aylesbury Bucks
Printed in Great Britain by
Robert Hartnoll (1985) Ltd, Bodmin

CONTENTS

Introduction

It may seem odd that someone whose work involves spending a good part of each day in the kitchen should have written a book about weekend cooking; the fact is, however, that my interest in food goes beyond my professional involvement and I find preparing family meals a welcome change from giving demonstrations and testing recipes. Nowadays, I make an effort to keep weekends free, giving everyone a much needed break from the Monday to Friday routine of alarm clocks, snatched meals and rush-hour travelling. I find that the nicest weekends are those spent at home pottering around the house and garden. Like a holiday, a weekend ought to have a special flavour, something which makes it stand out from the humdrum round of everyday life – and what better than a series of gastronomic delights? This may include an indulgent breakfast in bed, an impromptu picnic on the lawn, a formal dinner party or traditional Sunday lunch – no matter what the occasion, the emphasis is on enjoyment.

When one isn't hidebound by the weekday necessity for quick filling dishes, buying provisions can be fun. This is the time for browsing in speciality shops, experimenting with whatever takes your fancy and visiting local markets. On Saturday mornings, markets are brash and bursting with life, in stark contrast to the typical supermarket. One has to contend with a certain amount of jostling, especially in the vicinity of popular stalls, but at least the elbows are less hazardous than supermarket trolleys. The stallholders, warming up for the business of the day, begin vying for customers and you need to be alert to avoid being fobbed off with over-ripe fruit and woody vegetables. Experienced shoppers develop a keen eye for a bargain and learn not to trust a stallholder's gleaming display any more than his patter. I thoroughly enjoy this type of shopping; my list lies forgotten in the bottom of the basket as I cast my eyes over the range of produce, buying a quarter of this and half a pound of that, not sure what I'll do with everything when I get home but anticipating the intriguing possibilities.

I always make sure that I take home a selection of 'convenience foods': cheeses, cooked meats, fresh pasta, smoked fish, exotic fruits and unusual vegetables; foods which can be turned into delicious meals in a matter of minutes, for even I don't relish the thought of being tied to the stove all weekend. I prefer to concentrate my efforts on one or two meals, losing myself in the kitchen with a pile of ingredients and my favourite recipe books for guidance. The results of my endeavours don't always live up to expectations but they are certainly never dull. The best are included in this book: some are out of the ordinary while others are based on traditional dishes from home and abroad, and there is plenty to please both meat eaters and vegetarians alike. All reflect my simple approach to cooking which is uncomplicated and unpretentious, using fresh wholesome ingredients, without superfluous sauces or garnishes. Not only are lighter, less formal meals healthier but they also require less effort to prepare, leaving the cook free to relax and enjoy the weekend too. Finally, if skimmed milk and low-fat cheeses are required or preferred, these can easily be substituted as appropriate within relevant recipes.

Friday Evening

For many people, Friday night is a time for relaxing after the week's frenzied activities. Perhaps the previous week has been so hectic that all you want to do is spend a quiet evening at home or maybe you have to rush out to the local supermarket before meeting friends. In any event, it is unlikely that you will have either the time or inclination to spend hours slaving over a hot stove preparing a lavish meal, but Friday night deserves to be celebrated with more than a plate of beans on toast and it is an ideal time to try something a little out of the ordinary. Egg, pasta and fish dishes are obvious choices as they can be cooked quickly but it is also a good opportunity to experiment both with the wok and the pressure cooker, particularly when cooking stir-fried dishes and soups.

Stir-frying is the gourmet's answer to convenience foods. Not only is it quick and easy in terms of preparation but there are so many delicious combinations of foods which can be cooked in a wok that it would be possible to eat a different dish every day of the year. Although a large frying pan can be used, it is worth while investing in a wok if you make stir-fries regularly. One Chinese cook has described stir-fried dishes as 'hot salads' and this seems to sum up their qualities perfectly. The ingredients used should be fresh, varied and colourful, have contrasting textures and shapes, and be tossed in a piquant 'dressing' before being taken to the table.

While stir-fried dishes are cooked in a matter of minutes, pressure cooked dishes take longer but are no less useful to the busy cook. All manner of dishes can be cooked in about one-third of their normal cooking time, and the pressure cooker is particularly useful when preparing soups and stews. In the 1940s Doris Lytton Toye wrote, 'The pressure cooker opens up a whole new outlook on cooking and adds new zest to the kitchen. The cooker's compactness and cleanliness are excellent points, and it has a wonderful way of cooking a variety of food at the same time (disposed in racks) without losing or mixing any of the flavours. To the late homecomer with little time to cook, a pressure cooker is just manna from heaven. The technique is very simple and you have only to read and absorb the perfectly clear instructions to realize that the cooker, correctly handled, is positively foolproof. You couldn't blow yourself up if you tried.' (*Food in Vogue*, ed. Barbara Tims, Harrap 1976).

RICH CHEDDAR SOUP

A smooth, rich soup which is sufficiently filling to be served as a main course with plenty of bread, and followed by a green salad or fresh fruit.

Serves 3–4

1 large potato, diced	275 ml (½ pint) milk
1 large onion, chopped	100 g (4 oz) mature
1 carrot, diced	Cheddar cheese, grated
1 stick of celery, chopped	freshly ground black pepper
425 ml (¾ pint) chicken	1–2 tablespoons finely
stock (see page 156)	chopped fresh chives

Put the potato, onion, carrot, celery and chicken stock in a pan, and bring to the boil. Cover and simmer for 15 minutes, or pressure-cook at *high* pressure for 5 minutes. Pass the vegetables through a vegetable mouli or blend in a liquidizer or food processor until fairly smooth. Return to the pan and put over a gentle heat. Add the milk and grated cheese, and stir until the cheese has melted and the soup is heated through. Do not boil. Season to taste with black pepper. Spoon into individual dishes and sprinkle the chives over the top.

CREAMY ONION SOUP

I have been making this soup since my student days when my kitchens were hardly bigger than a hall cupboard and my *batterie de cuisine* consisted of little more than a kettle, pan, fork and spoon. It is, as you might expect, quick and easy to prepare, requiring no 'fancy' ingredients, and yet it looks and tastes exceedingly good and can be served with aplomb to friends and special visitors alike.

Serves 4

40 g (1½ oz) butter	850 ml (1½ pints) milk
3 large onions, finely	3 egg yolks
chopped	salt, pepper

Melt the butter in a large pan, and gently sauté the onions for 10-12 minutes until soft and golden-brown. Remove from the heat, and gradually stir in the milk. Return to the stove, and bring to a slow boil. Remove from the heat, then gradually stir in the egg yolks. Season to taste. Serve with granary rolls.

FINNAN HADDOCK SOUP

Serves 4

450 g (1 lb) Finnan haddock
1 onion, finely chopped
275–425 ml (½–¾ pint) milk
175 g (6 oz) potato, cooked

freshly ground black pepper
25 g (1 oz) butter, diced
 (optional)

Put the fish into a pan, skin side down, and barely cover with water.
Bring to a slow boil, reduce the heat, cover and poach for 5-6 minutes.
Lift from the pan and, when cool enough to handle, remove the skin
and bones. Reserve the cooking liquid. Return the fish to a clean pan
with 275 ml (½ pint) of the cooking liquid and the chopped onion, and
cook for a further 4–5 minutes. Add most of the milk and the potato.
Pass through the coarse blade of the vegetable mouli or blend in a
liquidizer or food processor until smooth. (I generally pass the soup
through a mouli and then liquidize about half of it. This way I obtain
both a thick, creamy soup and one which contains some texture.) Add
more milk if necessary. Season to taste with black pepper, then heat
through. Stir in the butter before serving, if using it.

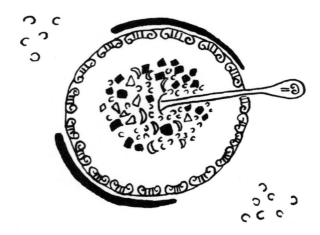

NEWFOUNDLAND CHOWDER

Like the Mediterranean bouillabaisse, the chowder is a cross between a fish soup and a stew and can be eaten with a spoon or a knife and fork. Scallops are rarely cheap for they are classed as one of the world's finest shellfish, having a firm texture and wonderful flavour. It is still fairly difficult to find scallops in their shells, but shelled ones are becoming an increasingly common sight at the fishmonger's. Most have been frozen but, fortunately, this doesn't seem to affect their flavour or texture too much.

Serves 4

1–2 tablespoons sunflower oil
175 g (6 oz) lean unsmoked bacon, trimmed and chopped
3 sticks of celery, chopped
4 potatoes, diced
4 carrots, diced

575 ml (1 pint) milk
350 g (12 oz) shelled scallops, halved
grated rind and juice of 1 orange
1–2 tablespoons finely chopped fresh parsley
freshly ground black pepper

Heat the oil in a casserole-type pan, and sauté the bacon and celery for 4–5 minutes. Add the potatoes and carrots, and cook for 3–4 minutes more, stirring frequently. Stir in the milk and bring to a slow boil. Cover and simmer gently for 12–15 minutes until the vegetables are soft. Add the scallops and the grated rind and juice of the orange, and poach for 3–5 minutes until the scallops are tender. Season to taste with parsley and black pepper. Serve with hot garlic bread (see page 14).

TOMATO AND HARICOT BEAN SOUP

A delicious late summer soup. The inclusion of haricot beans gives it more body than many other tomato soups. It can be made quickly in a pressure cooker.

Serves 4

100 g (4 oz) haricot beans, soaked overnight and then drained
850 ml (1½ pints) chicken stock (see page 156) *or* water
1 onion, chopped
1 stick of celery, chopped
1 clove of garlic, peeled and crushed
2 carrots, chopped
450 g (1 lb) ripe tomatoes, chopped
1 tablespoon tomato purée
salt, pepper

Using a large pan or pressure cooker, boil the beans briskly in the stock or water for at least 10 minutes, then add the remaining ingredients *except* for the seasoning. Cover and simmer for 1¼–1½ hours until the beans are tender, adding more stock or water as and when necessary, or pressure-cook at *high* pressure for 15 minutes. Pass the ingredients through a vegetable mouli or lightly blend in a liquidizer or food processor until smooth. Adjust the seasoning and consistency to taste. Serve with wholewheat bread.

GARLIC BREAD

Serves 4-6

225 g (8 oz) butter
6 cloves of garlic, peeled and crushed
1 French stick

Cream the butter with a wooden spoon until soft. Add the garlic, and mix together well. Cut the bread into slices, taking care not to cut through the base, then carefully spread both sides of each slice with the garlic butter. Press together, and wrap in foil. Bake in a preheated oven, gas mark 6 (200°C/400°F), for 20 minutes. Remove the foil, then return the loaf to the oven for a further 10 minutes to crisp up.

VEGETABLES PAYSANNE

A colourful and flavoursome vegetable casserole. Ideal for serving on a warm summer's evening with a glass of chilled white wine.

Serves 4–6

1–2 tablespoons olive oil
1 onion, chopped
2 cloves of garlic, peeled and crushed
100 g (4 oz) lean unsmoked bacon, trimmed and chopped
1 red pepper, chopped
1 aubergine, chopped
450 g (1 lb) ripe tomatoes, chopped

450 g (1 lb) courgettes, sliced
175 g (6 oz) mange-tout peas *or* French beans, trimmed and sliced if necessary
1 sprig of fresh rosemary
1 sprig of fresh oregano
1 sprig of fresh marjoram
75–125 ml (3–4 fl oz) water
salt, pepper

Heat the oil in a large casserole-type pan, and sauté the onion, garlic and bacon for 4–5 minutes. Add the remaining ingredients, cover and bring to the the boil. Simmer for 20–25 minutes, stirring occasionally, until the vegetables are tender and the stock well flavoured. Discard the herbs, and season to taste. Serve with potatoes, brown rice or bread rolls.

NITSUKE VEGETABLES

Nitsuke is a term used to describe vegetables which have been lightly stir-fried and then steamed until tender. It is an admirable method of cooking an assortment of vegetables in a wok as it ensures that even the harder root vegetables have the opportunity to soften.

Serves 4

1 tablespoon groundnut oil
1 onion, thinly sliced
1 red pepper, thinly sliced
¼ small cauliflower, broken
  into florets
2 carrots, cut into julienne
  strips
1 clove of garlic, peeled and
  crushed
2.5 cm/1 inch fresh root
  ginger, peeled and grated

2 courgettes, thinly sliced
100 g (4 oz) bean sprouts
2–3 teaspoons shoyu soya
  sauce
4 tablespoons water
a dash of dry white wine
  (optional)
1 bunch of watercress,
  trimmed and chopped

Heat the oil in a wok, toss in the onion and pepper, and stir-fry for 2–3 minutes. Add the cauliflower, carrots, garlic and ginger, and cook for several minutes more, stirring often. Add the courgettes and bean sprouts, then pour the soya sauce, water and wine over, if using it. Cover and simmer gently until the vegetables begin to soften. Place the watercress on top of the other vegetables, cover again and cook for 1–2 minutes more until the watercress has wilted. Serve immediately with rice or noodles.

Friday Evening

Tofu

Tofu has been a basic food in Japan and China for hundreds of years and is eaten in all manner of dishes. It is made from ground soya beans which are cooked in water and a souring agent. The resultant curds are then drained and pressed. Sold in slices or slabs, tofu is creamy white in colour and has a smooth firm texture, rather like a well-set junket. Fresh tofu should be kept cool and moist. In health food and wholefood shops it is usually sold in prepacked polythene wrappers from the refrigerator, whereas in Chinese delicatessen one is more likely to find it languishing in the bottom of a plastic bucket bathed in an opaque liquid. When I last bought some, the Chinese shop assistant fished out the squares of tofu and a generous amount of the liquid with a ladle and poured them into a plastic bag. This was sealed at the top and I carried it home as if it were some freakish goldfish won at a fair!

There are two types of tofu on sale in Britain today. That found in Chinese food stores is usually firm-pressed with a fairly solid consistency. It can be sliced without fear of it disintegrating, and is ideal for using in stir-fries. Firm tofu can also be bought in wholefood and health food shops but here one is more likely to find boxes of Silken tofu. This variety is much softer and does not slice neatly. It is best used for blending into mousses, sauces and soups and can be used as a substitute for yoghurt or cream. Although bland by nature, tofu readily absorbs the flavours of other foods. Do not be misled by its uninspiring appearance – tofu is very nutritious. It is high in complete protein, low in calories and fat, and free from cholesterol.

TOFU WITH STIR-FRIED VEGETABLES

Serves 4

100 g (4 oz) firm tofu, chopped into 0.6 cm (¼ inch) cubes
60 ml (2½ fl oz) shoyu soya sauce
1–2 teaspoons sesame oil
1 large onion, chopped
1 clove of garlic, peeled and crushed
1.25 cm (½ inch) fresh root ginger, peeled and grated

2 carrots, thinly sliced
2 sticks of celery, thinly sliced
100 g (4 oz) button mushrooms, halved if necessary
225 g (8 oz) broccoli, broken into florets
225 g (8 oz) tomatoes, chopped
60 ml (2½ fl oz) water

Put the chopped tofu into a small bowl. Pour the soya sauce over and leave for 20–30 minutes. Drain well and reserve the tofu and 2–3 teaspoons of the soya sauce. Heat the oil in a wok or large frying pan, and sauté the onion for 2–3 minutes. Add the garlic, ginger, carrots and celery, and stir-fry for several minutes more. Add the remaining vegetables, then pour over the water and the reserved soya sauce. Place the tofu on top of the vegetables, bring to the boil, cover and simmer gently until the vegetables are just tender. Serve with brown rice, noodles or buckwheat spaghetti.

BLACK EYE BEANS IN BEER

Another bean dish which can be cooked in under 30 minutes in a pressure cooker. Black eye beans do not need soaking before being cooked. The stew is richly flavoured and makes a hearty meal.

Serves 4

1–2 tablespoons sunflower oil
1 onion, chopped
225 g (8 oz) white turnip, chopped
225 g (8 oz) swede, chopped
225 g (8 oz) flat mushrooms, chopped
425 ml (¾ pint) bitter beer
425 ml (¾ pint) water

175 g (6 oz) black eye beans
½ level teaspoon ground cinnamon
½ level teaspoon ground cloves
1 tablespoon tomato purée
1 tablespoon shoyu soya sauce
freshly ground black pepper

Heat the oil in a large pan or pressure cooker, and gently sauté the onion for 5 minutes. Add the turnip, swede and mushrooms, and cook for several minutes more, stirring frequently. Pour the beer and water over, then add the beans, cinnamon, cloves and tomato purée. Cover and bring to the boil. Simmer for 1¼ hours or until the beans are tender. Add more water and beer if necessary but the stock should be fairly thick and rich-tasting at the end of the cooking period. If using a pressure cooker, pressure-cook at *high* pressure for 15 minutes, then reduce the pressure, uncover and boil briskly for 10 minutes, stirring occasionally until the stock thickens. Add the soya sauce, and season to taste with black pepper. Serve with boiled potatoes and a green vegetable – spinach is a particularly good choice.

MIXED VEGETABLE HOTPOT

Serves 4–6

100 g (4 oz) haricot beans, soaked overnight and then drained
850 ml (1½ pints) water
2 carrots, chopped
2 parsnips, chopped
1 stick of celery, chopped
100 g (4 oz) white cabbage, chopped
450 g (1 lb) potatoes, chopped

450 g (1 lb) ripe tomatoes, chopped
100 g (4 oz) French beans, trimmed and sliced
100 g (4 oz) shelled peas
2 sprigs of fresh thyme
2 sprigs of fresh parsley
1 sprig of fresh mint
1 bay leaf
salt, pepper

Using a large pan or pressure cooker, boil the haricot beans briskly in the water for at least 10 minutes, then add the other ingredients, cover and simmer for 1¼–1½ hours until tender, adding a little more water if necessary, or pressure-cook at *high* pressure for 15 minutes. Remove the herbs, and season to taste. Serve with wholewheat bread.

COURGETTE AND CANNELLINI CASSEROLE

This dish can be made with haricot beans but their flavour is not as good as that of the cannellini. Whichever you choose, it is essential to cook the beans until the skins are beginning to split open and the inside is soft.

Serves 4

175 g (6 oz) cannellini beans, soaked overnight and then drained
575 ml (1 pint) water
350 g (12 oz) courgettes, sliced

225 g (8 oz) lean unsmoked bacon, trimmed and chopped
4 tablespoons olive oil
1–1½ tablespoors white wine vinegar
freshly ground black pepper

Using a large pan or pressure cooker, boil the beans briskly in the water for at least 10 minutes. Cover and simmer for 1¼–1½ hours until tender, adding more water if necessary, or pressure-cook at *high* pressure for 14–15 minutes. Drain and reserve the stock. Put some of the stock in a small pan, add the courgettes, and simmer for 4–5 minutes until barely tender. Drain well.

Sauté the bacon in a heavy frying pan until lightly cooked – there should be no need to add any fat provided that you stir the bacon frequently. Add the cooked beans and courgettes, then remove from the heat. Mix together the oil and vinegar, and pour this over the bean mixture while it is still hot. Season with black pepper. Serve with new potatoes and grilled tomatoes.

TAGLIATELLE WITH FRESH HERBS AND PINE KERNELS

The success of this dish relies upon the use of fresh herbs – dried varieties simply will not do. Imported fresh herbs are becoming available all year round in high-class greengrocers and large supermarkets but they tend to be rather expensive. It is often better to wait until midsummer when the herbs in the garden are fragrant and ready to pick.

Serves 4

450 g (1 lb) wholewheat tagliatelle	50 g (2 oz) pine kernels
4–5 tablespoons olive oil	15 g (½ oz) fresh basil, finely chopped
50 g (2 oz) butter	15 g (½ oz) fresh oregano, finely chopped
2 onions, finely chopped	grated Parmesan cheese
2 cloves of garlic, peeled and crushed	

Fill a large pan with boiling water, then add the tagliatelle. Cook briskly for 10–12 minutes until *al dente*. Drain well and keep warm if necessary.

Meanwhile, make the sauce. Heat together the oil and butter in a frying pan, and sauté the onion and garlic for 5–7 minutes until soft and golden. Finely chop half the pine kernels, and stir into the pan along with the whole nuts. Stir-fry for several minutes until they begin to brown. Add the herbs and mix well. Put 3–4 tablespoons of the herb mixture to one side before carefully mixing in the cooked tagliatelle. Put on to a large hot serving dish and sprinkle the remaining herb mixture over the top. Serve immediately with a bowl of grated Parmesan cheese.

GIUSEPPE'S VEGETARIAN SPAGHETTI SAUCE

Dark, rich and full of flavour, this sauce is popular with vegetarians and meat-eaters alike.

Serves 4

2–3 tablespoons olive oil
2 onions, chopped
2 cloves of garlic, peeled and crushed
900 g (2 lb) ripe tomatoes, chopped

450 g (1 lb) flat mushrooms, sliced
½ teaspoon dried basil
½ teaspoon dried oregano
freshly ground black pepper

Heat the oil in a heavy-bottomed pan, and sauté the onion for 5–7 minutes until soft and golden. Add the garlic and tomatoes and cook for a further 3–4 minutes. Put the mushrooms, basil and oregano into the pan, cover and cook gently for 30–35 minutes until soft and fairly thick. Season to taste with black pepper.

Serve with wholewheat spaghetti or tagliatelle.

SPAGHETTI WITH MUSHROOMS AND CORIANDER

Wholewheat spaghetti topped with a deliciously creamy sauce.

Serves 4

50 g (2 oz) butter
2 onions, finely chopped
2 cloves of garlic, peeled and
   crushed
450 g (1 lb) button
   mushrooms, sliced
juice of 2 lemons
2 good pinches of ground
   coriander

450 g (1 lb) low-medium fat
   cream cheese
3-4 tablespoons natural
   yoghurt
450 g (1 lb) wholewheat
   spaghetti

Melt the butter in a pan, and sauté the onion and garlic for 5–7 minutes until soft and golden. Stir in the mushrooms and cook for several minutes more. Pour the lemon juice over and season to taste with coriander. Cover and cook for a further 7–8 minutes over a low heat.

Meanwhile, fill a large pan with boiling water, then add the spaghetti. Cook briskly for 10–12 minutes until *al dente*. Drain well and keep warm.

Mix together the cream cheese and yoghurt until smooth, and stir into the cooked mushrooms. Heat gently and pour over the pasta before serving. Serve immediately with a crisp green salad.

SPECKLED RICE WITH TWO CHEESES

I don't often cook brown rice in a pressure cooker as, although the cooking time is reduced, the rice tends to be rather sticky and is not appropriate for every dish. Stickiness does not, however, present a problem in this particular recipe – if anything, it is a positive advantage. Speckled Rice with Two Cheeses is an Italian dish and, traditionally, the rice would have been cooked slowly and lovingly to give it the creamy texture of a risotto. The addition of grated cheese just before serving adds to these qualities as well as providing flavour.

Serves 4

2-3 tablespoons olive oil
1 onion, finely chopped
275 g (10 oz) long grain
  brown rice
725 ml (1¼ pints) water
juice of 1 lemon
225 g (8 oz) Gruyère cheese,
  grated

25 g (1 oz) Parmesan cheese,
  grated
2 level tablespoons finely
  chopped fresh parsley
1 level teaspoon dried basil
freshly ground black pepper

Heat the oil in a pressure cooker or heavy-based pan, and sauté the onion for 5-7 minutes until soft and golden. Add the rice, and sauté for 1-2 minutes more. Pour the water over and pressure-cook at *high* pressure for 12 minutes, or cover and simmer gently for 30-35 minutes. When the rice is tender, stir in the lemon juice, and cook, uncovered, stirring all the time until the surplus moisture has been driven off. Stir in the grated cheeses, parsley and basil, and season to taste with black pepper. Serve immediately, accompanied by wine, crusty bread and a colourful vegetable dish such as French Beans with Tomatoes and Peppers (see page 71).

OEUFS MARCEL

A delicious combination of courgettes, spinach, Gruyère and Parmesan cheeses topped with eggs.

Serves 4

2-3 tablespoons olive oil
1 onion, chopped
450 g (1 lb) spinach,
   trimmed, rinsed and
   chopped
2 cloves of garlic, peeled and
   crushed
450 g (1 lb) courgettes,
   grated

75 g (3 oz) Gruyère cheese,
   grated
4 eggs
freshly ground black pepper
1-2 tablespoons grated
   Parmesan cheese

Heat the oil in a large, heavy frying pan, and sauté the onion for 5-7 minutes until soft and golden. Put the spinach into a separate pan, cover and cook gently for 8-10 minutes, without adding any water, until tender. Drain well.

Stir the crushed garlic and grated courgettes into the sautéed onions, and cook for 3-4 minutes, stirring frequently. Add the spinach, and continue to cook for a minute or two more. Stir in the grated Gruyère cheese and then, space permitting, make four hollows in the mixture, each about 6.25 cm (2½ inches) in diameter, and break an egg into each. Cook until the eggs have set. Sprinkle with black pepper and Parmesan cheese. Serve immediately, with sautéed potatoes.

Note: If your pan is not large enough to hold the eggs, poach them separately, and place them on top of the vegetable mixture before taking to the table.

CHINESE VEGETABLES WITH PRAWNS

Serves 4

3 tablespoons groundnut oil
2 leeks, thinly sliced
1 red pepper, thinly sliced
1 clove of garlic, peeled and
  crushed
2.5 cm (1 inch) fresh root
  ginger, peeled and grated

100 g (4 oz) button
  mushrooms, sliced
100 g (4 oz) bean sprouts
2 teaspoons shoyu soya sauce
100 g (4 oz) peeled prawns

Heat the oil in a wok, toss in the leeks and pepper, and stir-fry for 2–3
minutes. Add the garlic, root ginger and mushrooms, and cook for 1–2
minutes. Stir in the bean sprouts, soya sauce and prawns, and cook
briefly until the prawns are heated through. Serve with brown rice or
noodles.

STIR-FRIED DOVER SOLE

A light and delicately flavoured dish which is equally good served with
brown rice or noodles.

Serves 4

2 small–medium Dover sole,
  filleted and skinned
2 tablespoons sesame oil
1 tablespoon lemon juice
450 g (1 lb) courgettes,
  sliced

100 g (4 oz) button
  mushrooms, sliced
1–2 tablespoons shoyu soya
  sauce

Cut the fish into narrow strips, about 2.5 cm (1 inch) long. Put into a
small bowl and pour over 1 tablespoon each sesame oil and lemon juice.
Mix together gently, cover and leave to marinate for 30 minutes. Drain
well.

Heat the remaining oil in a wok and stir-fry the courgettes for 3–4
minutes. Toss in the mushrooms and cook for a minute or two more.
When the courgettes are almost tender, add the marinated fish, and
stir-fry for a minute or so before pouring over the soya sauce. Cook
quickly until the fish is tender. Serve immediately.

DEVILLED HADDOCK

Serves 4

a good knob of butter
550–675 g (1¼–1½ lb)
 haddock fillets, skinned
1–2 tablespoons Dijon
 mustard

25–50 g (1–2 oz) fresh
 wholewheat breadcrumbs
salt, pepper

Spread a little of the butter in the base of a shallow ovenproof dish. Brush the haddock with the mustard before placing in the dish. Cover with the breadcrumbs, and dot with the remaining butter. Season to taste. Bake in a preheated oven, gas mark 5 (190°C/375°F), for 15–20 minutes until golden-brown. Serve with sautéed potatoes and spinach or grilled tomatoes.

HADDOCK CRISP

Lightly poached haddock and vegetables with a low-fat crunchy topping.

Serves 4

550–675 g (1¼–1½ lb)
 haddock fillets, skinned
 and cut into large pieces
juice of 1 lemon
100 g (4 oz) button
 mushrooms, sliced
2 tomatoes, sliced

1 tablespoon chopped fresh
 parsley
salt, pepper
75 g (3 oz) fresh wholewheat
 breadcrumbs
75 g (3 oz) natural cottage
 cheese

Place the pieces of fish in an ovenproof dish. Pour the lemon juice over and lay the sliced mushrooms and tomatoes on top. Sprinkle with parsley, and season to taste. Mix together the breadcrumbs and cottage cheese and then scatter them over the vegetables. Bake in a preheated oven, gas mark 6 (200°C/400°F), for 20–25 minutes until the fish is tender and the topping golden-brown.

COD BAKED WITH YOGHURT AND HERBS

Serves 4

butter as required
550–675 g (1¼–1½ lb) cod
   fillets, skinned
275 ml (½ pint) natural
   yoghurt

1–2 tablespoons chopped
   fresh herbs (parsley, chives
   and tarragon)

Spread a little butter in an ovenproof dish. Place the fish in the dish. Pour the yoghurt over, and sprinkle the herbs on top. Bake in a preheated oven, gas mark 4 (180°C/350°F), for 25 minutes until the fish is tender.

VENETIAN'S DELIGHT

This superb recipe contains three of my favourite ingredients – globe artichokes, scallops and prawns. Rather than throwing away the leaves (or petals) of four perfectly good artichokes, which seems a terrible waste considering their price, I usually make this dish when my greengrocer has a supply of cheap, less than perfect specimens.

A light meal for 4

2–3 tablespoons olive oil
1 large onion, finely chopped
4 globe artichokes
1 crisp lettuce, outer leaves
   removed and shredded
175 g (6 oz) shelled peas,
   blanched if not young and
   tender

3 tablespoons dry white wine
100 g (4 oz) peeled prawns
100 g (4 oz) shelled scallops,
   sliced
salt, pepper

Heat the oil in a large, heavy casserole-type pan, and gently sauté the onion taking care not to brown. Meanwhile, prepare the artichokes, quickly trimming each one in turn as the flesh discolours when exposed to the air. First, cut off the stalk close to the head, remove the tough outer leaves and slice off and discard the top half of each artichoke. Now, cut the trimmed artichoke in half from top to bottom. Remove the thistle-like choke with a sharp knife, and thinly slice what remains

– the heart. Put into the pan with the onion, and repeat until all the artichokes have been prepared in this fashion. Add the lettuce, handful by handful, stirring well after each addition, until it begins to wilt, then add the peas and wine. Cover and simmer gently for 7–10 minutes until the vegetables are beginning to soften. Stir in the prawns and scallops, cover again, and cook gently for 4–5 minutes until heated through and tender. Season to taste. Serve immediately with new potatoes or crusty bread and a good white wine.

CHICKEN WITH HERBS IN FOIL

A delicious recipe that came originally from Arabella Boxer's book, *The Herb Book* (Octopus Books, 1980). I generally bone the chicken breasts and cut them in two to speed up the cooking time.

Serves 4

olive oil
2 tablespoons Dijon mustard
2 tablespoons natural
   yoghurt
4 chicken breasts, skinned,
   boned and cut into 2 fillets

salt, pepper
6 tablespoons chopped fresh
   herbs (parsley, chives,
   tarragon, chervil)
juice of 1 lemon

Brush four pieces of foil with olive oil. Mix together the mustard and yoghurt and use to coat the chicken pieces. Arrange each chicken breast on a piece of foil, season to taste and sprinkle some of the herbs and the lemon juice over the top. Fold the foil to form a loose but secure parcel. Bake in a preheated oven, gas mark 5 (190°C/375°F), for 20 minutes until the chicken is tender. Unwrap the four parcels, taking care not to spill any of the cooking juices. Pour these over the chicken before taking to the table. Serve with new potatoes and a green salad or vegetable.

CAPONATA WITH SQUID

I must admit that preparing squid is not one of my favourite pastimes but I have perfected a method which is quick, straightforward and relatively clean. For this Sicilian recipe, choose medium-sized squid, about 10–15 cm (4–6 inches) in total length, for the larger the creature the longer it will take to cook. Some squid are sold still shrouded in their veil-like translucent skin, irregularly mottled with pinkish grey patches. It covers the body but is easily peeled away. Also remove the skin from the two fins before pulling them from the body.

To prepare the squid, first locate the tentacles, the sac-like body with its two fins and the narrow head lying between the two. Cut off the tentacles close to the head, and place aside. Take hold of the head in one hand and the body in the other. Pull the two sections gently apart. The viscera, including the ink sac, will come away with the head and can be discarded. The sac-like body will now be empty except for the quill and a little mucous membrane. Locate the end of the transparent quill, grasp it by the tip, pull free and discard. Rinse the body under cold running water, and, using the fingertips, carefully pull away the remaining membrane from inside the body. Rinse the squid's tentacles, fins and sac-like body, and pat dry. They are now ready for use.

Serves 4

450 g (1 lb) squid	2 tablespoons white wine
2–3 tablespoons olive oil	vinegar
1 onion, chopped	12 green olives, stoned
4 sticks of celery, thinly sliced	2 tablespoons chopped fresh
1 large aubergine, thinly	parsley
sliced, then chopped into	salt, pepper
bite-sized pieces	
450 g (1 lb) ripe tomatoes,	
chopped	

Prepare the squid as directed above. Cut into slices about 0.6 cm (¼ inch) wide. Set aside.

Heat the oil in a large, casserole-type pan, and sauté the onion and celery for 5–7 minutes until they begin to soften. Add the chopped aubergine and tomatoes, and continue to cook for several minutes more, stirring frequently. Add the wine vinegar, olives, parsley and squid, cover and simmer gently for 20–25 minutes until the vegetables are tender. Season to taste. Serve with fresh bread or potatoes.

STIR-FRIED STEAK WITH LEMON

Serves 4

1–2 tablespoons sunflower
oil
1 large onion, chopped
2 cloves of garlic, peeled and
crushed
350 g (12 oz) sirloin steak,
trimmed and thinly sliced
100 g (4 oz) button
mushrooms, sliced

1 green pepper, sliced
¼ teaspoon chilli powder
2 level teaspoons ground
cumin
juice of 2 lemons
275 ml (½ pint) water
salt, pepper

Heat the oil in a wok or large frying pan, and sauté the onion and garlic
for 5–7 minutes until they begin to soften. Meanwhile, place the meat
between two sheets of greaseproof paper. Beat with a meat tenderizer
or rolling-pin until the meat is fairly thin. Cut into delicate strips. Toss
the meat into the pan, and stir-fry for several minutes until brown on all
sides. Add the mushrooms, pepper, chilli powder and ground cumin.
Pour the lemon juice and water over, and bring to the boil. Cover and
simmer for 15–20 minutes until the meat is tender. Season to taste, and
serve with brown rice.

LEEK AND HAM ROLLS

When buying leeks late in the season (in April and May), test one or two to check that they are sound since the central core sometimes becomes hard and woody. Care must be taken, too, to remove all the grit and dirt which may be trapped between the layers as cleaning whole leeks can be tricky. Trim the tops and roots, remove any coarse outer leaves, then stand the leeks, root end uppermost, in a large jug of water for 30 minutes. Rinse carefully. If the leeks are particularly dirty, or you are short of time, slit them open down one side and rinse well, letting the water run through the layers.

Serves 4

8 thin leeks, trimmed and cleaned	FOR THE SAUCE
	15 g (½ oz) butter
8 slices of cooked ham	1 tablespoon sunflower oil
butter as required	25 g (1 oz) unbleached white flour
	275 ml (½ pint) milk
	1 teaspoon Dijon mustard
	freshly grated nutmeg

Steam the leeks until barely tender. When cool enough to handle, wrap a slice of ham around each one. Arrange in the base of a lightly buttered ovenproof dish.

To make the sauce, heat together the butter and oil in a saucepan, and stir in the flour. Cook for a minute or two until the mixture begins to bubble. Remove from the heat, then gradually add the milk, stirring well after each addition. Return to the heat and bring to the boil, stirring all the time, until the sauce thickens. Add the mustard, and season to taste with nutmeg.

Pour the sauce over the rolled leeks, and bake in a preheated oven, gas mark 6 (200°C/400°F), for 20–25 minutes until heated through.

PORK CHOPS WITH FENNEL AND CIDER SAUCE

A refreshing change to the more usual combination of pork and apple.

Serves 4

2 sticks of celery, chopped
1 Florence fennel bulb,
   chopped
3 tablespoons sunflower oil

1 heaped tablespoon
   unbleached white flour
275 ml (½ pint) dry cider
salt, pepper
4 pork chops, trimmed

Put the celery and fennel in a small pan, barely cover with water, and bring to the boil. Cover and simmer for 3–4 minutes. Drain well.

Heat 2 tablespoons of the oil in a clean pan, and sauté the parboiled vegetables for several minutes. Stir in the flour, and cook gently until the mixture begins to bubble. Remove from the heat, then gradually add the cider, stirring well after each addition. Return to the heat and bring to the boil, stirring all the time, until the sauce thickens. Season to taste.

Meanwhile, brush the chops with the remaining oil, and cook under a hot grill for 7–10 minutes on each side until tender. Serve with the fennel and cider sauce.

GINGER CHOPS

Serves 4

2 tablespoons groundnut oil
2 cloves of garlic, peeled and
   crushed

3.75 cm (1½ inches) fresh
   root ginger, peeled and
   grated
4 lamb chops, trimmed
oil as required

Mix together the oil, garlic and ginger in a small bowl. Place the chops on an oiled grill rack. Brush liberally with the garlic mixture, and cook under a hot grill for 6–8 minutes. Turn over, brush the other side of the chops with the remaining mixture, and cook for a further 6–8 minutes until tender. Serve with potatoes and a green vegetable or salad.

SPAGHETTI 'BOLOGNESE'

A dish extended with beans, both economical and richly flavoured.

Serves 4

100 g (4 oz) brown lentils	1 bay leaf
275 ml (½ pint) water	a good pinch of mixed dried
1–2 tablespoons vegetable oil	herbs
1 large onion, finely chopped	1–2 teaspoons yeast extract
225 g (8 oz) minced beef	1 tablespoon tomato purée
400 g (14 oz) canned plum	freshly ground black pepper
tomatoes, chopped	

Sort through the lentils and remove any small stones or pieces of grit. Put into a large pan and pour the water over. Cover and simmer for 50–60 minutes, adding more water as and when necessary, until the lentils are soft. If using a pressure cooker, cook at *high* pressure for 12 minutes. Drain well.

Heat the oil in a large frying pan, and fry the onion lightly until beginning to brown. Add the minced beef, and fry until that, too, begins to brown. Add the tomatoes, cooked lentils and the bay leaf. Season to taste with dried mixed herbs, yeast extract, tomato purée and freshly ground black pepper. Cover and simmer for 25–30 minutes until the meat is tender and the sauce is thick. Serve with wholewheat spaghetti.

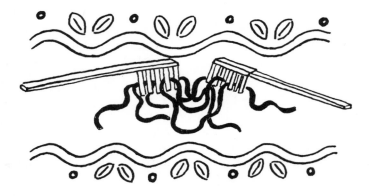

Offal

One has only to visit the 'butcher's row' in the markets of northern England to realize that there is more to offal than liver. Dotted amongst the stalls selling familiar cuts of beef, coils of sausages, trays of stewing steak and sides of bacon is a much rarer breed of butcher, one whose wares look decidedly strange and unappetizing to the uninitiated. Labels identifying lights, tripe, chitterlings, sweetbreads and udders don't always help, although most people are aware that they refer to the internal organs of an animal, and for a good many this is reason in itself to avoid them.

In spite of my northern upbringing, my attitude to offal is somewhat more reserved than that of my hardier compatriots, and I don't share their enthusiasm. No amount of coaxing and cajoling could persuade me, as a child, to try one of my father's favourite dishes, tripe and onions, but at least he was not as devious in his attempts as a group of Indian ladies who invited me to lunch. As their English was limited and my Gujarati non-existent, I wasn't unduly surprised or concerned when I couldn't find out what it was I was being given to eat. My enjoyment of the meal, however, came to an abrupt halt halfway through when, amid much giggling, I was told that the two principal ingredients were sheep's brains and goat's intestines. I am ashamed to say that my stomach did several somersaults, and I felt the blood drain from my face but I did finish the meal, albeit with less enthusiasm and gusto than when I started.

My reaction was not uncommon, for many people baulk at the idea of eating offal. It is a pity that we react in this way as offal can be very tasty and is both highly nutritious and reasonably cheap. While it would be hypocritical of me to suggest that we all ought to eat more offal, I can, with all honesty, sing the praises of liver and kidney, both of which I really do enjoy eating.

LIVER WITH YOGHURT AND THYME

Serves 4

1–2 tablespoons olive oil
1 onion, chopped
450 g (1 lb) lambs' liver, cut into slices 1.25 cm (½ inch) thick and 5 cm (2 inches) long
275-350 ml (10–12 fl oz) natural yoghurt

1 tablespoon tomato purée
1–2 tablespoons chopped fresh thyme
1 tablespoon wholewheat flour
salt, pepper

Heat the oil in a large frying pan, and sauté the onion for 5–7 minutes until soft and golden. Add the liver, and brown lightly, turning frequently. Mix together the remaining ingredients, and pour them over the liver. Stir well and bring to the boil. Simmer gently for 8–10 minutes until the liver is tender. Season to taste.

LAMBS' LIVER WITH PARSLEY

This dish is particularly quick and easy to make – so much so that you need to have the rest of the meal almost ready before starting to cook the liver.

Serves 4

2–3 tablespoons olive oil
450 g (1 lb) lambs' liver, thinly sliced
2 cloves of garlic, peeled and crushed
150 ml (¼ pint) dry white wine

2 tablespoons white wine vinegar
3–4 tablespoons chopped fresh parsley
salt, pepper

Heat the oil in a frying pan, and sauté the liver for 4–6 minutes, turning occasionally until barely tender. Add the garlic, stirring well. Pour the wine and wine vinegar over, and leave the stock to bubble for a minute or two. Stir in the parsley, and season to taste. Serve immediately.

SWEET AND SOUR LIVER

An unusual recipe well worth making. Use pineapple chunks steeped in natural juice rather than heavy syrup.

Serves 4

2-3 tablespoons sunflower oil
1 large onion, chopped
1 large green pepper, chopped
2 cloves of garlic, peeled and crushed
2.5 cm (1 inch) fresh root ginger, peeled and grated
225 g (8 oz) canned pineapple chunks in natural juice, drained (juice reserved)

150 ml (¼ pint) white wine vinegar
1-2 tablespoons tomato purée
200-225 ml (7-8 fl oz) natural unsweetened orange juice
2-3 tablespoons shoyu soya sauce
freshly ground black pepper
450 g (1 lb) lambs' liver, cut into thin strips

Heat 1-2 tablespoons of oil in a frying pan, and sauté the onion for 4-6 minutes until soft and golden. Add the pepper, garlic and ginger, and cook for several minutes more. Add the pineapple chunks and wine vinegar, and bring to the boil. Simmer until only 2-3 tablespoons of liquid remain, then stir in the tomato purée. Pour the reserved pineapple juice into a measuring jug, and add sufficient orange juice to bring the amount up to 275 ml (½ pint). Stir this juice into the pan, then blend in a liquidizer or food processor until smooth. Season to taste with soya sauce and black pepper.

Wash out the frying pan, and return to the heat. Heat the remaining oil, and toss the liver into the pan. Fry quickly until tender. Pour the sweet and sour sauce over the top, and stir well before serving.

KIDNEYS ROYALE

Supplies of lambs' kidneys are often limited and may not be on display at the butcher's. It pays to ask. Sometimes they come encased in a layer of firm, white fat which is removed along with the white skin before cooking.

Serves 4

½-1 tablespoon sunflower oil
175 g (6 oz) lean unsmoked
   bacon, trimmed and
   chopped into bite-sized
   pieces
1 onion, finely chopped
10 lambs' kidneys, halved

150 ml (¼ pint) dry white
   wine
4-6 tablespoons water
freshly grated nutmeg
1-2 tablespoons chopped
   fresh chives

Heat a little of the oil in a large, heavy pan, and sauté the bacon and onion for 5-6 minutes until soft and golden. Add the kidneys and sauté gently for 5-7 minutes until almost tender. Pour the wine over and bring to the boil. Simmer gently for a minute or two, turning the kidneys occasionally. Stir well to loosen any meat juices which may have stuck to the base of the pan. If necessary, thin down the stock with the water so that there is sufficient gravy to serve with the kidneys. Season to taste with nutmeg. Spoon into a serving dish, and sprinkle with the chives before taking to the table.

Saturday Morning

BREAKFASTS AND SNACKS

potato cakes

omelets

Saturday Morning

Snacks and savouries have largely replaced the midday meal. Saturday lunchtime, in particular, has changed beyond all recognition since my childhood, with Welsh rarebit, buttered mushrooms on toast, sandwiches and pizzas replacing the meat and two veg.. Although most people are at home on a Saturday, it is often far more hectic than the preceding five days, and meals have to be fitted in between trips to the shops, the occasional DIY job, washing and gardening.

Historically, savouries were small, strongly flavoured, hot dishes served at the end of a lengthy dinner. It was a uniquely British tradition and one which was generally associated with the Victorian era. Nowadays, a savoury is occasionally served after the sweet but it is more usual to find it appearing as a snack food at lunchtimes. To be honest, I don't regret the demise of the after-dinner savoury for I find even a three-course meal sufficient for my modest appetite, but it is reassuring to see that the recipes themselves have survived the passage of time and have found a new lease of life in what is quite decidedly a late-twentieth-century meal – the casual and often hurried lunch.

The food manufacturers have responded to the needs of the busy cook by providing a variety of convenience foods which require little, if any, preparation or cooking. Unfortunately, many of these products have received a bad press because of their high levels of fat, salt, sugar and chemical additives with the result that some people feel positively guilty about using them. However, there really is no reason why we should not eat and enjoy the occasional plate of fish and chips or fish fingers, the odd pie or hamburger, tin of beans or spaghetti rings, particularly if the rest of one's diet is sound and contains lots of starchy carbohydrates, high fibre foods, fruit and vegetables and only moderate amounts of fatty meat and dairy products. The foods we should be avoiding are, perhaps, those brimming over with additives, but, once again, it must be a question of balance and commonsense. The use of chemicals in the production of livestock, poultry, vegetables and cereals makes it extremely difficult to eliminate them entirely from our diet, but selective buying and the close scrutiny of labels can result in a fairly dramatic reduction.

Pre-packed foods may be convenient but they are certainly inferior to home-made dishes. Don't let us forget either that many savoury and snack foods can be prepared equally quickly from ingredients found in the average refrigerator or larder as is demonstrated in this chapter.

VEGETABLE AND EGG FRICASSEE

A traditional savoury dish that has been updated to meet our increasing desire for healthier foods. The original seventeenth-century recipe included 275 ml (½ pint) cream.

Serves 4

50 g (2 oz) butter
2 large onions, chopped
2 cloves of garlic, peeled and crushed
225 g (8 oz) button mushrooms, sliced
2 heaped teaspoons unbleached white flour

275 ml (½ pint) milk
2 tablespoons lemon juice
2 tablespoons chopped fresh parsley
freshly ground black pepper
4 hard–boiled eggs, cut into quarters
4 slices wholewheat toast

Melt the butter in a pan, and sauté the onions and garlic until soft and golden. Add the mushrooms, and cook for a further 3–4 minutes. Stir in the flour and let the mixture bubble. Remove from the heat, then gradually add the milk, stirring well after each addition. Return to the heat, and bring to the boil, stirring all the time, until the sauce thickens. Thin down with more milk if necessary. Season to taste with lemon juice, parsley and black pepper. Carefully fork the egg quarters into the mixture, spoon this over the slices of wholewheat toast, and serve immediately.

TOMATOES AU GRATIN

Serves 4

4 medium-large tomatoes
1 tablespoon sunflower oil
1 onion, finely chopped
100 g (4 oz) button mushrooms, chopped
2 egg yolks
1 tablespoon chopped fresh parsley

salt, pepper
2 tablespoons fresh wholewheat breadcrumbs
1–2 tablespoons grated Parmesan cheese

Slice the top from each tomato and scoop out the pulpy centre, taking care not to break through the skin. Chop the discarded flesh and put aside with the hollowed-out tomatoes until needed.

Heat the oil in a frying pan, and sauté the onion for 5–7 minutes, taking care not to brown. Add the mushrooms, and continue to cook for several minutes more. Stir in the chopped tomato, and sauté until the vegetables begin to soften. Remove from the heat and stir in the egg yolks and parsley. Season to taste.

Stand the hollowed-out tomatoes on a baking tray, and fill with the vegetable mixture. Scatter the breadcrumbs over the top, and sprinkle with the Parmesan cheese. Bake in a preheated oven, gas mark 7 (220°C/425°F), for 15-20 minutes until tender. Serve with whole-wheat toast.

EGGS FLORENTINE

An attractive dish consisting of a layer of tender spinach with four poached eggs nestling in its midst. A smooth, creamy sauce is poured over, and it is taken to the table bubbling hot and golden-brown.

Serves 4

450 g (1 lb) spinach, trimmed and rinsed
50 g (2 oz) butter
100 g (4 oz) button mushrooms, sliced
40 g (1½ oz) unbleached white flour
425 ml (¾ pint) milk
75 g (3 oz) Gruyère cheese, grated
freshly grated nutmeg
4 eggs

Shake off some of the surplus water from the spinach before putting into a large pan. Cook over a moderate to low heat until tender. Drain well. Chop coarsely, then keep warm until needed.

Melt the butter in a saucepan, and sauté the mushrooms for 2-3 minutes. Stir in the flour and let the mixture bubble. Remove from the heat, then gradually add the milk, stirring well after each addition. Return to the heat and bring to the boil, stirring all the time, until the sauce begins to thicken. Add the grated cheese, and season to taste with nutmeg.

Meanwhile, poach the eggs. Place the cooked spinach in the base of an ovenproof dish. Lay the poached eggs on top, and pour the sauce over. Place under a hot grill until the sauce is bubbling and beginning to brown. Serve with sautéed potatoes or wholewheat toast.

Omelets

The omelet has become something of a legend over the years, and pages and pages of advice have been written on how to make the perfect dish. Some cooks go to such lengths that it can take longer to read and digest their instructions than it does to prepare and eat the omelet itself.

A French lady, calling herself Mère Poulard, who is reputed to have had theatrical leanings, did much to renew interest and enthusiasm in this essentially homely dish. She ran a restaurant on the island of Mont-St-Michel, just off the coast of Normandy, where every day without exception her customers sat down to a meal of omelets, ham, fried sole, lamb cutlets with potatoes, a roast chicken, a salad, a dessert and finally coffee. It wasn't the bounteous menu which drew the crowds but the great lady's omelets. Their reputation spread far and wide, and controversy raged as to why they were so light and creamy. It was claimed that she added cream to the eggs, cooked them in a special long-handled pan which was never washed and even used eggs from a rare breed of hen. Her reply to all this speculation was, '*Je casse de bons oeufs dans une terrine. Je les bats bien, je mets un bon morceau de beurre dans le poele, j'y jette les oeufs et je remue constamment.*'

She was, of course, quite right; there is nothing more to making an omelet than beating the eggs and cooking them in a hot pan, but to make a good omelet requires a little more skill. Choose a flat-bottomed, heavy pan that is the right size for the number of eggs being used. My cast-iron pan is about 15 cm (6 inches) in diameter and holds two large eggs. It is an ideal size for a 'one man' omelet. Beat the eggs lightly with a fork, adding nothing more than a little seasoning. Preheat the pan so that the small knob of butter used to coat the bottom melts and froths as soon as it is added. Unsalted butter will reduce the risk of it browning and burning. Pour the eggs into the pan, and gently lift the edges of the omelet as soon as it begins to firm up, allowing the uncooked mixture to trickle underneath. This will all take a matter of moments, for a good omelet should be the same soft, light consistency throughout and not be left in the pan until the bottom is leathery and well browned.

The basic omelet has been greatly modified and adapted over the years, and nowadays one finds it stuffed with lobster, wrapped around asparagus spears, enriched with double cream, beaten to resemble a soufflé, dredged in sugar, and served with jam. Although these creations can be delicious, they are seldom as good as a simple *omelette fines herbs*. Not for the first time I find myself agreeing with Elizabeth David who says, 'What one wants is the taste of the fresh eggs and the fresh butter and, visually, a soft bright golden roll, plump and spilling out a little at the edges. It should not be a busy, important urban dish but something gentle and pastoral, with the clean scent of the dairy, the kitchen garden, the basket of early morning mushrooms, or the sharp tang of freshly picked herbs.'

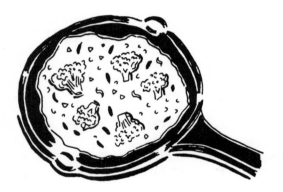

OMELETTE FINES HERBES

Serves 1

a small knob of butter
2 large eggs, beaten
1 level teaspoon finely
  chopped fresh parsley
1 level teaspoon finely
  chopped fresh chives

1 level teaspoon finely
  chopped fresh chervil
½ tablespoon grated
  Parmesan cheese
freshly ground black pepper

Preheat a small, heavy frying pan before adding the butter. When it has melted, pour in the beaten eggs, and scatter the herbs on top. Cook the omelet quickly, allowing the uncooked eggs to run underneath. Lightly sprinkle with Parmesan cheese and season with black pepper. Fold in half, then slide on to a plate. Serve immediately.

STUFFED OMELET CHINESE-STYLE

Serves 1

1 tablespoon sesame seeds
100 g (4 oz) frozen spinach,
  defrosted and chopped
2 eggs

1–2 teaspoons shoyu soya
  sauce
a small knob of butter

Put the sesame seeds into a pan, and cook over a high heat, shaking the pan frequently, until they begin to pop and jump about. Add the spinach, and cover the pan. Reduce the heat and cook gently for 5–6 minutes, stirring occasionally to ensure that the contents of the pan do not burn. Cover and keep warm.

Beat together the eggs and soya sauce. Preheat a small, heavy frying pan and add the butter. When it has melted, pour in the eggs. Cook the omelet quickly, allowing the uncooked eggs to run underneath. Spread the spinach mixture over the top. Fold in half, and serve immediately.

COURGETTE AND GRUYÈRE OMELET

A subtle combination of textures, flavours and colours that makes the perfect filling.

Serves 1

15 g (½ oz) butter
1 courgette, grated
2 large eggs, beaten

40 g (1½ oz) Gruyère cheese,
  grated

Preheat a small, heavy frying pan. Melt the butter and sauté the grated courgette for several minutes until it just begins to soften. Lift from the pan with a slotted spoon and keep warm.

Pour the eggs into the pan, and cook the omelet quickly, allowing the uncooked eggs to run underneath. Sprinkle the grated cheese and cooked courgettes over the top. Fold in half, and serve immediately.

VEGETABLE OMELET

Serves 1

15 g (½ oz) butter	1 tomato, chopped
1 stick of celery, finely chopped	1 tablespoon chopped fresh parsley
2-3 button mushrooms, chopped	salt, pepper
	2 large eggs, beaten

Preheat a small, heavy frying pan. Melt half the butter and sauté the celery for several minutes until it begins to soften. Add the mushrooms and tomato, and cook until they also soften. Stir in the parsley, and season to taste. Remove from the pan and keep warm.

Toss the remaining butter into the pan, and when it begins to melt, pour in the eggs. Cook the omelet quickly, allowing the uncooked eggs to run underneath. Spread the vegetable filling over the top, fold the omelet in half, and serve immediately.

SOUFFLÉ OMELET WITH BROCCOLI AND MUSHROOMS

Serves 2

salt, pepper	50 g (2 oz) button mushrooms, chopped
100 g (4 oz) broccoli, broken into florets	2 large eggs, separated
15 g (½ oz) butter	

Season the broccoli, then steam until barely tender. Put into a small bowl.

Meanwhile, melt half the butter in a frying pan, and sauté the mushrooms for several minutes until cooked. Remove from the pan, then put into the bowl with the broccoli. Stir in the egg yolks. Beat the egg whites until stiff, then fold into the mixture. Preheat a grill.

Toss the remaining butter into the frying pan, and heat until it begins to foam. Pour in the omelet mixture, spread the top evenly, and cook for a minute or so until the bottom has begun to set. Place the pan under the hot grill, and continue to cook until the top is set and lightly browned. Cut in half, and slide on to plates. Serve immediately.

POTATO CAKES

An ideal snack food. Potato cakes are easy to make and filling. It is important to make and cook the mixture quickly as the grated potatoes brown rapidly once exposed to the air.

Serves 4

675 g (1½ lb) potatoes, scrubbed
1 small onion, finely chopped
1 teaspoon chopped fresh rosemary

1 egg, beaten
2 rounded tablespoons unbleached white flour
salt, pepper
sunflower oil

Working quickly, grate the potatoes, and put into a bowl with the onion. Add the rosemary, beaten egg and flour, and season to taste. Heat 2-3 tablespoons of oil in a frying pan, and using half the potato mixture, place four mounds in the pan. Flatten gently with a fish slice or palette knife, and cook on both sides until golden-brown. Drain on absorbent paper, and keep warm while cooking the remaining four potato cakes. Serve with grilled tomatoes or baked beans and poached eggs.

GLAMORGAN SAUSAGES

Serves 4

150 g (5 oz) Lancashire *or* Caerphilly cheese, grated
150-175 g (5-6 oz) fresh wholewheat breadcrumbs
3-4 tablespoons finely chopped spring onion *or* leek
2 eggs, separated

2 tablespoons chopped fresh parsley
½ teaspoon dried mixed herbs
1 teaspoon ready-made English mustard
freshly ground black pepper
sunflower *or* soya oil

Mix together the cheese, 100 g (4 oz) of the breadcrumbs, the spring onion or leek. Add the egg yolks, herbs and mustard, and season to taste with black pepper. Divide into 12 pieces and roll out like sausages, about 5 cm (2 inches) long. Beat the egg whites lightly, and dip the 'sausages' first in this, then roll in the remaining breadcrumbs. Fry in 1.25 cm (½ inch) hot oil or bake in a preheated oven, gas mark 6 (200°C/400°F), for 15-20 minutes until lightly browned. Serve with cooked tomatoes.

CHEESE AND POTATO PIE

One weekend last summer while helping friends to move house, I rashly offered to cook the evening meal so as to leave them free to collect the last of their belongings. Although I hadn't expected to find a well-stocked larder, I was more than a little taken aback to discover that the provisions consisted of a piece of cake, some potatoes, an onion, jars of peanut butter and jam, a loaf of bread, a slab of cheese, a can of peas, and a can of beans. Left without transport, I couldn't even pop over to the village shop which was several miles away, and to add to my problem I was also catering for two small girls whose preference was quite definitely for chips. Just as I was about to give up all pretence of cooking a meal and to settle for things on toast, I remembered the cheese and potato pies of my student days. I hadn't made one for years and was more than a little surprised to rediscover how good they could be. The addition of some baked beans guaranteed success with the children too.

Serves 4

1 tablespoon sunflower oil	175 g (6 oz) Cheddar cheese,
1 large onion, finely chopped	grated
675 g (1½ lb) potatoes,	salt, pepper
cooked and mashed	400 g (14 oz) canned baked
	beans (optional)

Heat the oil in a frying pan, and sauté the onion until soft and golden. Place in a mixing bowl with the mashed potatoes and most of the grated cheese. Mix together well, and season to taste. Spoon the beans, if using them, into the base of an ovenproof dish, and cover with the potato mixture. Scatter the remaining cheese on top, and bake in a preheated oven, gas mark 6 (200°C/400°F), for 25-30 minutes until lightly browned and heated through.

TOMATO MACARONI CHEESE

Serves 3–4

175 g (6 oz) wholewheat
  macaroni

FOR THE SAUCE
25 g (1 oz) butter
2 tablespoons sunflower oil
50 g (2 oz) unbleached white
  flour

425 ml (¾ pint) milk
½ teaspoon ready-made
  English mustard
4 tomatoes, chopped
175 g (6 oz) mature
  Cheddar cheese, grated
freshly ground black pepper

Fill a large pan with boiling water, then add the macaroni. Cook briskly for 10–12 minutes until *al dente*. Drain well.

Meanwhile, make the sauce. Heat together the butter and oil in a pan, and stir in the flour. Cook for a minute or two until the mixture begins to bubble. Remove from the heat, then gradually add the milk, stirring well after each addition. Return to the heat and bring to the boil, stirring all the time, until the sauce thickens. Add the mustard powder, chopped tomatoes and most of the grated cheese. Season to taste with black pepper.

Place the macaroni in an ovenproof dish. Pour the sauce over, and mix together well. Sprinkle the remaining cheese over the dish, and place in a preheated oven, gas mark 6 (200°C/400°F), for 20–25 minutes until the sauce is heated through and bubbling.

EGGY BREAD WITH BACON

Serves 4

225 g (8 oz) lean unsmoked
  bacon, trimmed
8 slices of wholewheat bread

mustard to taste
2 large eggs, beaten
sunflower oil

Lightly fry the bacon. Make four sandwiches with the bread and cooked bacon, using mustard to taste. Pour the beaten eggs in a shallow bowl or pie plate, and dip both sides of each sandwich into the mixture. Fry quickly in the pan, adding a little oil if necessary. Serve immediately. This is very good eaten with cooked tomatoes or mushrooms.

SMOKED MACKEREL AND MUSHROOM AU GRATIN

Serves 3–4

2 smoked mackerel fillets,
  each weighing 150 g
  (5 oz), skinned and flaked
2 tablespoons sunflower oil
100 g (4 oz) button
  mushrooms, sliced
1 rounded tablespoon
  unbleached white flour

225 ml (8 fl oz) milk
2 tablespoons natural
  yoghurt
freshly grated nutmeg
grated rind of 1 lemon
25 g (1 oz) fresh wholewheat
  breadcrumbs
butter as required

Put the fish in an ovenproof dish. Heat the oil in a pan, and sauté the mushrooms, for 4-5 minutes. Stir in the flour and let the mixture bubble. Remove from the heat, then gradually add the milk, stirring well after each addition. Return to the heat and bring to the boil, stirring all the time, until the sauce thickens. Add the yoghurt, and season liberally with nutmeg. Pour this over the fish, and mix together gently. Sprinkle the grated lemon rind and breadcrumbs over the top. Dot with butter, and bake in a preheated oven, gas mark 6 (200°C/400°F), for 20 minutes until heated through and lightly browned.

Herrings

In our attempts to reduce the quantity of fat in our diet, it is often overlooked that some fats are essential for good health. Not only are they a source of energy, but they are also needed for the building and repair of cells, particularly those of the brain, nervous system and vascular tissues. One of the cheapest and richest sources of these essential fatty acids is oily fish such as herring (including kippers, bloaters and buckling), mackerel, sprats and whitebait. Herrings are also a good source of protein, iodine and vitamins A and D. They are the most common oily fish and are generally available all year round, although at their best from midsummer to late October. Choose firm, plump fish whose eyes, gills and scales are bright and shiny.

To prepare a herring, cut open its belly and clean out the viscera. Remove the head and fins. On a work surface or chopping board, spread the body open, skin side uppermost, and press down gently but firmly along the backbone. Turn the fish over and ease out the backbone, taking with it as many of the smaller bones as possible, and breaking it off at the tail. The fish is now ready to cook.

GRILLED HERRINGS

When grilling fish the principles are the same as for meat. The fish is first painted with oil or butter and then put under a hot grill for a minute or two before the heat is reduced and the cooking continued at a slower pace. The skin of the fish is usually crisped up under the hot grill, but try to resist the temptation to turn the fish too often, and always handle it carefully using tongs, a fish slice, palette knife or double-sided, two-handed grill specifically designed for the purpose.

Cooking times obviously vary from fish to fish but as a rule, fillets take less time and require a less fierce heat than a whole plump herring. Whole fish, weighing more than 175 g (6 oz), should be scored with two or three deep cuts on both sides to allow the heat to penetrate the thicker, fleshier parts and to ensure even cooking. Always keep a watchful eye on the grill while cooking, as a minute or two can make all the difference between a perfectly cooked fish and a dry, overcooked one. Cook until the flesh is opaque and comes away from the bone.

FRIED HERRINGS

The traditional coatings of flour, oatmeal, egg and breadcrumbs, and batter not only offer the fish some protection from the searing heat but also make them easier to handle, improve their appearance and flavour and stop them absorbing too much oil. The fish, however, should be no more than 2.5 cm (1 inch) thick otherwise they will not cook through in the time it takes for the coating to become crisp and golden-brown. The best cooking fats are clarified butter and vegetable oils, particularly groundnut and corn oil, as they both have high smoking points.

SCOTTISH-STYLE HERRINGS

Clean and trim the herrings, dip in milk, and roll in coarse oatmeal. Heat a pan containing a little fat (traditionally dripping) until it begins to give off hazy blue smoke. The fat should come about halfway up the fish. Put the fish into the pan, and cook very quickly for several minutes on both sides until lightly browned and tender. Drain well and serve immediately with tomatoes and bread and butter.

DRY PAN FRYING

In order to cut down on fat, I seldom fry foods these days but I find this method a particularly useful and appetizing way of dealing with small oily fish such as herrings. Heat a lightly oiled, heavy-bottomed frying pan, and place the fish on the base – they must lay flat in a single layer. Cook for 4–6 minutes on each side until tender and lightly browned.

KIPPER SCRAMBLE

Serves 2–3

1 kipper
butter as required
4 eggs, beaten

freshly ground black pepper
wholewheat toast

Place the kipper, head first, in a jug of boiling water. Leave to stand for 4–6 minutes. Lift out and drain well. When cool enough to handle, remove the skin and bones, and divide the flesh into flakes. Keep warm until needed.

Melt a knob of butter in a small pan, and add the eggs. Stir occasionally until lightly cooked. Gently mix in the flaked kipper, and season with black pepper. Spoon the mixture over buttered wholewheat toast, and serve immediately.

SARDINE AND COTTAGE CHEESE SNACK

Serves 4

75 g (3 oz) canned sardines
   in oil, drained
75 g (3 oz) natural cottage
   cheese

freshly ground black pepper
4 slices of wholewheat bread
1 large tomato, thinly sliced

Put the sardines into a small bowl. Mash with a fork, then stir in the cottage cheese. Season to taste with black pepper. Toast the bread on one side only. Spread the sardines and cottage cheese mixture over the untoasted side of each slice, and top with 2–3 slices of tomato. Put under a hot grill, and cook for several minutes until heated through.

SARDINE ROLLS

Makes 8

FOR THE PASTRY
225 g (8 oz) wholewheat
  flour
75 g (3 oz) butter, diced
2 tablespoons sunflower oil
8 teaspoons cold water

FOR THE FILLING
8 canned sardines in oil *or*
  brine, drained

100 g (4 oz) mature
  Cheddar cheese, grated
3 tablespoons chopped fresh
  parsley
freshly ground black pepper
beaten egg
2 tablespoons grated
  Parmesan cheese

To make the pastry, put the flour in a mixing bowl, and rub in the butter and oil, using the fingertips, until the mixture resembles breadcrumbs. Add the water, and mix to form a pastry dough. Roll out on a lightly floured board to 0.6 cm (¼ inch) thickness. Cut into eight rectangles measuring approximately 7.5 × 5 cm (3 × 2 inches).

Lay a sardine down the middle of each pastry rectangle, and sprinkle with a little grated Cheddar cheese and parsley. Season with black pepper. Roll up like a Swiss roll, and seal the edges. Place on an oiled baking tray, and brush with beaten egg. Sprinkle the Parmesan cheese over the top, and bake in a preheated oven, gas mark 6 (200°C/400°F), for 25 minutes until golden-brown. Serve warm or cold.

CAYENNE KIDNEYS

Serves 4

8 lambs' kidneys, halved
2–3 teaspoons Dijon
  mustard
½ teaspoon Cayenne pepper

freshly ground black pepper
1–2 tablespoons sunflower
  oil

Secure the kidneys on to an oiled skewer in such a way that they will not curl up during cooking. Mix together the mustard and Cayenne pepper in a small bowl, and season with black pepper. Brush the mixture over the kidneys. Place on a lightly oiled grill pan, and brush with the sunflower oil. Cook under a hot grill for 5–7 minutes, turning once. Serve with grilled tomatoes and mushrooms.

Saturday Evening
ENTERTAINING

Raspberry Sorbet

Soufflés

Watercress & Bacon Salad

Saturday Evening

Much has been written about the art of entertaining but the best advice of all is to keep the occasion simple and to avoid excessive effort. Of course, inviting guests for a meal invariably involves extra work but there is nothing to be gained from being pretentious or extremely formal. The current trend is towards lighter foods and fewer courses but this does not necessarily mean that the meal will be any easier to prepare than an *haute cuisine* menu. It is well worth paying a little more attention to detail when laying the table and selecting serving dishes, but the finest china and silver will not make up for any deficiencies in the meal itself. Nor is it the time to experiment with new recipes or to try and introduce your guests to the delights of tripe, mussels or goatsmilk yoghurt unless you are sure that they will rise to the challenge. It is always best to choose dishes that you yourself enjoy cooking and eating and to let the quality of the food and relaxed atmosphere speak for themselves.

Marcel Boulestin, the popular gourmet, restaurateur and cookery writer who made his home in London, brought a lot of French wisdom and commonsense to the English table in the 1920s and '30s, and his ideas on entertaining were no exception. He believed strongly in the importance of good food and the mellowing effect of a leisurely meal, and, to this end, he detested, firstly, being given a strong drink two seconds before being asked to sit down to dinner, plus smoking between courses and hurried meals. 'A meal worth eating', he said, 'must take at least an hour and a half; apart from the fact that it is not healthy to eat quickly, there is the other point of view with which we are concerned – the point of view of the pleasure of the table, to which leisure, anticipation and enjoyment contribute equally.'

Starters

MUSHROOM AND CORIANDER SOUP

Serves 4

1-2 tablespoons olive oil
5 shallots, finely chopped
450 g (1 lb) button
    mushrooms, chopped
425 ml (¾ pint) chicken *or*
    water (see page 156)

425 ml (¾ pint) milk
25 g (1 oz) butter
25 g (1 oz) wholewheat flour
1-2 tablespoons ground
    coriander
juice of 1 lemon
freshly ground black pepper

Heat the oil in a large pan, and gently sauté the shallots until they begin to soften, taking care not to brown them. Add the mushrooms, the stock and milk, then bring to the boil. Cover and simmer for 10-15 minutes. Pass through a vegetable mouli or blend in a liquidizer or food processor until fairly smooth.

Melt the butter in a pan, stir in the flour and let the mixture bubble. Remove from the heat, then gradually add the liquidized ingredients. Return to the heat, add the coriander and bring to the boil, stirring all the time, until the soup begins to thicken. Season to taste with lemon juice and black pepper.

SPICY PEANUT SOUP

An intriguingly flavoured soup that is deceptively rich and filling. Do leave yourself sufficient time to infuse the milk; a well-flavoured milk stock is essential to the success of the dish.

Serves 4–6

FOR THE STOCK
425 ml (¾ pint) milk
1 sprig of fresh parsley
¼ stick of celery, chopped
½ carrot, chopped
1 slice of onion
10 black peppercorns
4 green cardamom pods
4 coriander seeds
1 bay leaf
1 slice of lemon

FOR THE REMAINING INGREDIENTS
225 g (8 oz) smooth peanut butter
275–425 ml (½–¾ pint) water
2 teaspoons Madras curry powder
freshly ground black pepper
½–1 teaspoon garam masala

To make the stock, put all the ingredients in a pan, and bring to the boil. Remove from the heat, and leave to infuse for 20–25 minutes. Strain and reserve the milk.

Put the strained milk, the peanut butter and half the water in a bowl, liquidizer or food processor, and whisk or blend until smooth. Return to the pan, and adjust the consistency to taste with the remaining water. Stir in the curry powder, and season with black pepper. Heat through and, just before serving, stir in the garam masala. For a smoother soup, pass through a fine sieve before heating again.

CHICKEN AND YOGHURT SOUP

The success of this soup depends on the quality of the chicken stock, which should be home-made. It is customary to make stock with the bird's carcass and giblets but this assumes that one has enjoyed roast chicken the day before. If I were to roast a bird every time I needed some stock, I would be eating little else, so I tend to buy chicken wings or drumsticks specifically for the stock pot. They can be bought in most supermarkets and are very reasonably priced. After making the stock, trim the meat from the bones, chop into small pieces and stir into the soup.

Serves 4

FOR THE STOCK
4 chicken wings *or*
  drumsticks
150 ml (¼ pint) dry white
  wine
1.1 litres (2 pints) water
1 carrot, sliced
2 slices of onion
2 bay leaves
10 black peppercorns
2 sprigs of fresh parsley
2 sprigs of fresh thyme

FOR THE REMAINING INGREDIENTS
50 g (2 oz) bulgur wheat
275 ml (½ pint) boiling
  water
25 g (1 oz) butter
1 large onion, finely chopped
2 large leeks, thinly sliced
275 ml (½ pint) natural
  yoghurt
salt, pepper
2–3 tablespoons chopped
  fresh parsley

To make the stock, put all the ingredients in a large pan, bring to the boil and cover. Simmer gently for 20 minutes. Remove the chicken pieces and, when cool enough to handle, trim off and reserve the meat. Return the bones to the stock, cover and continue to cook for a further 10–15 minutes. Strain and discard the solids.

Put the bulgur wheat in a bowl, and pour over the boiling water. Leave to stand for 15–20 minutes.

Meanwhile, melt the butter in a large pan, and gently sauté the onion and leeks for 5–7 minutes until soft and golden-brown. Pour the chicken stock over the vegetables. Drain the bulgur wheat, and add to the pan together with the reserved chicken meat. Bring to the boil, and cook for several minutes. Spoon the yoghurt into a bowl, and stir in 3–4 ladlefuls of hot stock, then pour this mixture into the rest of the stock. Heat through gently, taking care not to boil. Season to taste, and sprinkle with parsley before serving.

LENTIL SOUP WITH APRICOTS AND CUMIN

A beautifully coloured soup with a delicate flavour.

Serves 4

50 g (2 oz) dried apricots
150 ml (¼ pint) boiling
 water
1 stick of celery, chopped
1 carrot, chopped
1 potato, chopped
50 g (2 oz) red lentils
2 sprigs of fresh thyme

juice of ½ lemon
1 litre (1¾ pints) water
1 level teaspoon ground
 cumin
2-3 tablespoons chopped
 fresh parsley
salt, pepper

Put the apricots in a small bowl, and pour the water over. Leave to soak for several hours until the apricots begin to soften.

Transfer the apricots and their liquid to a large pan or pressure cooker, and add the celery, carrot and potato. Sort through the lentils and remove any small stones or pieces of grit before adding to the pan together with the thyme, lemon juice, water and ground cumin. Bring to the boil and simmer gently for 50–60 minutes, or pressure-cook at *high* pressure for 10 minutes. When the lentils are soft, remove the thyme, and pass the soup through a vegetable mouli or blend in a liquidizer or food processor until smooth and creamy. Adjust the consistency to taste. Stir in the parsley, and season to taste before serving.

INDIVIDUAL CAULIFLOWER AND GRUYÈRE SOUFFLÉS

Serves 4-6

1 small cauliflower, broken
  into florets
40 g (1½ oz) butter
40 g (1½ oz) unbleached
  white flour
275 ml (½ pint) milk
150 ml (¼ pint) water
freshly grated nutmeg

1 level teaspoon English
  mustard powder
3 eggs, separated
freshly ground black pepper
50 g (2 oz) Gruyère cheese,
  grated

Put the cauliflower into a pan of boiling water, and cook until tender. Drain well.

Melt the butter in a saucepan, stir in the flour and let the mixture bubble. Remove from the heat, then gradually add the milk and water, stirring well after each addition. Return to the heat and bring to the boil, stirring all the time, until the sauce thickens. Add a little nutmeg and the mustard powder.

Pour the sauce into a large bowl, stir in the cooked cauliflower, and mix together well until it is broken into small pieces. Add the egg yolks, grated cheese, and season with pepper. Beat the egg whites until stiff and peaked, then fold them into the mixture. Spoon into four or six lightly oiled, individual soufflé or ramekin dishes, and bake in a preheated oven, gas mark 6 (200°C/400°F), for 20-25 minutes until well risen and firm to the touch.

Note: There is no need to surround the dishes with tall paper collars provided that each dish is not more than two-thirds full before cooking. Bake until golden-brown and just firm to the touch – soufflés should be moist and soft-textured in the centre.

EGGS IN A NEST

The recipe given makes more mayonnaise than is needed, but it will keep for a number of days in the refrigerator, and is delicious with many salads and other foods.

Serves 6

FOR THE MAYONNAISE
1 tablespoon sunflower oil
1 small onion, finely chopped
3 level teaspoons Madras
  curry powder
grated rind and juice of 1
  lemon
1 teaspoon tomato purée
150 ml (¼ pint) natural
  yoghurt
1 large egg
salt, pepper
½ level teaspoon English
  mustard powder

1 tablespoon white wine
  vinegar
200 ml (7 fl oz) sunflower oil
1-2 tablespoons hot water, if
  necessary

FOR THE REMAINING INGREDIENTS
6 round wholewheat rolls
a knob of butter
freshly ground black pepper
25-50 g (1-2 oz) peeled
  prawns
6 eggs

First, make the mayonnaise. Heat the tablespoon of oil in a pan, and gently sauté the onion until soft and golden. Add the curry powder, and cook for several minutes more, stirring frequently. Add the lemon juice, and continue to cook until it has been driven off. Stir in the grated lemon rind, tomato purée and yoghurt. Mix together well, then push through a sieve. Set aside until needed.

Put the egg into the goblet of a liquidizer or food processor, and season to taste. Add the mustard powder and 1 teaspoon of the white wine vinegar. Whizz at the lowest setting until smooth. Keep the machine operating while gradually pouring in the oil until it is all incorporated and the mayonnaise is thick and creamy. Pour into a bowl, then gently stir in the strained yoghurt mixture. If necessary, adjust the consistency and flavour of the sauce by adding more wine vinegar or some hot water to taste.

Cut the top from each roll, and scoop out the soft centre, taking care not to break through the crust. Make a cavity large enough to hold an egg. Spread the inside of each roll with butter, and season with black pepper. Place on a baking tray, and drop several prawns into the base of each hollow. Break an egg over the top, and bake in a preheated oven, gas mark 4 (180°C/350°F), for 10-15 minutes until the egg whites have set. Serve with the mayonnaise.

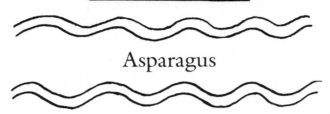

Asparagus

Asparagus has been prized for its delicate flavour for thousands of years but it has always ranked as a luxury food. Only the delicate young shoots of the plant are eaten. When in prime condition, asparagus heads or spears should be tightly compressed and firm to the touch. The stalk should look fresh and feel woody at the base only. Old asparagus tends to look dry and wrinkled with a somewhat limp, dejected appearance and is, therefore, best avoided.

When it comes to cooking asparagus, it is worth taking note of an old Roman proverb, '*velocium quam asparagi*', which is used when someone wants something done in a hurry, and, roughly translated, means 'do it in less time that it would take to cook asparagus'. One should avoid overcooking this vegetable; properly cooked it should be neither crunchy nor limp. If you are in the habit of eating a lot of asparagus, you will probably have already invested in an asparagus pan. For those of you who treat yourselves only once or twice a year, resourceful improvization is the key to success. You can, of course, use an ordinary steamer or cook the trimmed shoots in a pan of gently boiling water. Although boiling asparagus tends to be frowned upon, I don't find that it comes to too much harm, provided that it is cooked for the absolute minimum of time, often as little as 4-6 minutes. A more conventional way of cooking asparagus is to tie it up in even-sized bundles and to secure these in a vertical position by tying them to the handle of your deepest pan. Pour in sufficient boiling water to come about halfway up the asparagus stalks. Cover with a lid or a sheet of foil, and cook for 10-12 minutes until tender. The exact time will depend upon the age and thickness of the asparagus. Asparagus can also be cooked *en papillote*, in other words sealed inside a loose foil or greaseproof paper parcel with a knob of butter and a dash of lemon juice. Bake the parcel in a preheated oven, gas mark 4(180°C/350°F), for approximately 20 minutes. The spears should not be piled one on top of another but placed side by side in a row.

Before cooking asparagus, it must be cleaned and trimmed. First, rinse carefully to remove any grit and then trim off the bottom of each stalk where it becomes hard and woody. Some people prefer to skin the stalks, starting just below the tip. Certainly this removes the small leaves which may harbour grit but I think that it spoils the attractive appearance of the asparagus. Don't discard the trimmings or cooking water as they can be used to flavour soups. Similarly, it is a nice idea to cook some new potatoes in with the asparagus. Not only does this help to keep the asparagus upright but the asparagus, in turn, imparts its own delicate flavour to the potato.

ASPARAGUS WITH A CREAMY MUSHROOM SAUCE

Serves 4

450 g (1 lb) asparagus, cleaned and trimmed

FOR THE MUSHROOM SAUCE
150 ml (¼ pint) milk
1 egg
50 g (2 oz) button mushrooms, sliced
salt, pepper

Cook the asparagus as directed on page 63 until just tender.

Meanwhile, beat together the milk and egg, and place in a heavy-based pan. Add the mushrooms and heat gently over a low heat, stirring all the time, until the sauce begins to thicken. Do not bring to the boil. If the sauce separates, pour it into a liquidizer or food processor, and give it a few quick whizzes. Return to the pan, heat through very gently and season to taste. To serve, pour the sauce over the asparagus, and serve warm rather than hot.

ASPARAGUS AND PRAWN TART

A particularly attractive dish – the asparagus is arranged like the spokes of a wheel, pale green against a creamy yellow background. The prawns add a blush of colour.

Serves 4-6

FOR THE PASTRY
175 g (6 oz) wholewheat
  flour
75 g (3 oz) butter, diced
6 teaspoons cold water

FOR THE FILLING
8 spears of asparagus,
  cleaned and trimmed
150 ml (¼ pint) milk
2 eggs
salt, pepper
50 g (2 oz) peeled prawns
1-2 tablespoons grated
  Parmesan cheese

To make the pastry, put the flour in a mixing bowl, and rub in the butter, using the fingertips, until the mixture resembles breadcrumbs. Add the water, and mix to form a pastry dough. Roll out on a lightly floured board, and use to line a 20 cm (8 inch) flan ring. Prick the base with a fork and bake blind in a preheated oven, gas mark 6 (200°C/400°F), for 10 minutes. Meanwhile, cook the asparagus as directed on page 63 until barely tender.

Beat together the milk and eggs, and season to taste. Pour into the pastry case. Arrange the asparagus on top, like the spokes of a wheel, and then scatter the prawns in each segment. Sprinkle the Parmesan cheese over the top and return to the oven. Bake for a further 20-25 minutes until firm to the touch. Serve warm or cold.

BLUE STILTON AND ONION TARTS

Makes 12

FOR THE PASTRY
225 g (8 oz) wholewheat
  flour
75 g (3 oz) butter, diced
2 tablespoons sunflower oil
8 teaspoons cold water

FOR THE FILLING
2 tablespoons sunflower oil
1 large onion, chopped
100 g (4 oz) Blue Stilton
  cheese, crumbled
1 egg
60 ml (2½ fl oz) milk

To make the pastry, put the flour in a mixing bowl, and rub in the butter and oil, using the fingertips, until the mixture resembles breadcrumbs. Add the water, and mix to form a pastry dough. Roll out on a lightly floured board, and use to line 12 bun tins. Prick the pastry bases with a fork and bake blind in a preheated oven, gas mark 6 (200°C/400°F), for 8–10 minutes.

To make the filling, heat the oil in a frying pan, and sauté the onion for 5–7 minutes until soft and golden. Take care not to brown. Remove with a slotted spoon, and arrange in the base of the pastry cases. Sprinkle the cheese on top. Beat together the egg and milk, and spoon this over the cheese and onion. Return to the oven, and bake for a further 15–20 minutes until firm to the touch.

WATERCRESS AND BACON SALAD

Serves 4

100 g (4 oz) lean unsmoked
  bacon, trimmed
2 slices of wholewheat bread
1 clove of garlic, peeled
1 bunch of watercress,
  trimmed, washed and
  dried
50 g (2 oz) button
  mushrooms, sliced

FOR THE DRESSING
2 tablespoons olive oil
a scant 1 tablespoon white
  wine vinegar
a pinch of chilli powder
salt, pepper

Grill the bacon until tender. Chop into bite-sized pieces, and put into a salad bowl. Toast the bread, discard the crusts, and rub each side with the clove of garlic. Cut into cubes, and put on to a baking tray. Bake in a moderate–hot oven for 10 minutes until crisp. Toss into the salad bowl with the bacon. Add the watercress together with the sliced mushrooms.

To make the dressing, put the oil, vinegar and chilli powder in a screw-topped jar, and season to taste. Shake well. Pour this over the salad just before serving.

SALADE ARMORIQUE

Like the previous recipe, this salad has enough flavour and interest to be served as a course in its own right with crusty bread rolls and butter.

Serves 4–6

1 lettuce heart, chopped	1–2 tablespoons natural
1 Florence fennel bulb,	yoghurt
chopped	1–2 teaspoons walnut oil
1 eating apple, cored and	1–2 tablespoons chopped
chopped	fresh parsley
3 soft–boiled eggs	

Place the lettuce in a salad bowl with the fennel and apple. Cut the eggs in half, scoop out the fairly soft yolks and put them into a small bowl. Chop the whites, and toss with the salad vegetables. Blend the yoghurt and walnut oil with the yolks by hand or in a liquidizer or food processor to form a fairly smooth and creamy dressing. Sprinkle the parsley over the salad, then add the dressing, and toss well.

CAULIFLOWER AND HAM SALAD

Mark Twain described the cauliflower as 'nothing but a cabbage with a college education' while Elizabeth David, the doyenne of the English kitchen, damns it for its coarse flavour and soggy texture, and says that it is only good for making soup. Such dismissive words are not totally justified for as often as not the fault lies with the cook rather than the vegetable. While cauliflower may look robust, it needs handling with kid gloves as its texture becomes flaccid more quickly than you can say *Brassica oleracea*.

Serves 4

1 small cauliflower, broken into florets
100 g (4 oz) button mushrooms, sliced
100 g (4 oz) roast ham, chopped
3 tablespoons white wine vinegar

6 tablespoons cold pressed sesame oil
2 level teaspoons English mustard powder
1–2 tablespoons chopped fresh chives
freshly ground black pepper

Put the cauliflower into a pan of boiling water, and cook for 2–3 minutes until *al dente*. Drain well. Place in a mixing bowl with the mushrooms and ham. Mix together the wine vinegar, sesame oil and mustard powder, and pour this over the vegetables. Sprinkle the chives on top, and season with black pepper. Toss lightly. Cover and leave in a cool place for 45 minutes before serving with garlic bread (see page 14).

MELON, ORANGE AND WATERCRESS SALAD

Serves 4

½ honeydew melon, cubed
1 orange, peeled and
  chopped
1 bunch of watercress,
  trimmed and chopped

½ tablespoon white wine
  vinegar
a good pinch of English
  mustard powder
freshly ground black pepper

FOR THE VINAIGRETTE
1 tablespoon olive oil

Put the melon, orange and watercress in a bowl.

To make the vinaigrette, mix together the oil, wine vinegar and mustard powder, and season liberally with black pepper.

Pour the vinaigrette into the bowl, and toss the ingredients lightly. Serve with soft bread rolls.

Vegetable Dishes

STIR-FRIED CARROT AND CELERIAC

Celeriac is becoming an increasingly common sight in our green-grocers throughout the winter. It is a round, rough-skinned, root vegetable and, as the name suggests, its flavour is not unlike that of celery. Prepare and cook celeriac as if it were swede or turnip, but try to choose one with a relatively smooth skin in order to cut down on wastage. The cream-coloured flesh discolours quickly after being exposed to the air and, as soon as it has been peeled, should be put into water to which a dash of lemon juice or vinegar has been added.

Serves 4

2 teaspoons sesame oil
225 g (8 oz) carrot, grated
225 g (8 oz) celeriac, peeled
   and grated

juice of 1 orange
1–2 tablespoons sesame seeds

Heat the oil in a wok, and toss in the carrot and celeriac. Stir-fry for 2–3 minutes. Pour the orange juice over, and mix together. Add the sesame seeds, and stir once more before serving.

STIR-FRIED MANGE-TOUT PEAS

Serves 4

225 g (8 oz) mange-tout
   peas, trimmed
1 tablespoon sesame oil

1 crisp lettuce heart,
   shredded
1 tablespoon chopped fresh
   chives

Cook the mange-tout peas in a pan of boiling water for 2–3 minutes. Drain well. Heat the oil in wok, toss in the peas and lettuce, and stir-fry for 3–4 minutes. Sprinkle with chives, and serve immediately.

FRENCH BEANS WITH TOMATOES AND PEPPERS

Serves 4

1-2 tablespoons olive oil
1 onion, chopped
1 small green pepper, sliced
3 tomatoes, chopped

100 g (4 oz) French beans, sliced
3 tablespoons dry white wine
10 black olives, stoned
salt, pepper

Heat the oil in a pan, and sauté the onion and green pepper for 8–10 minutes until soft. Add the tomatoes, and cook for a further 5 minutes until they begin to soften. Stir in the remaining ingredients, then cover the pan, and simmer gently for 15–20 minutes until the beans are tender. Adjust the seasoning to taste before serving.

COURGETTE AND TOMATO AGRODOLCE

Serves 4

1-2 tablespoons olive oil
350 g (12 oz) courgettes, sliced
350 g (12 oz) tomatoes, chopped

3 tablespoons white wine vinegar
25 g (1 oz) pine kernels, lightly chopped
salt, pepper

Heat the oil in a frying pan, and fry the courgettes for a minute or two, then add the chopped tomatoes. Continue to cook, stirring frequently, until the courgettes are tender. Add the wine vinegar and pine kernels, and heat through. Season to taste before serving.

FENNEL WITH SAFFRON SAUCE

It is better to buy saffron strands than powdered varieties, for you can then be sure of getting the genuine product. There is no such thing as cheap saffron. It is hardly surprising that saffron is so expensive for it is estimated that only 30 tons are produced a year and that 70,000 blooms are needed to make 25 g (1 oz) of saffron.

I have read that saffron is harvested by men and women clad only in rough leather leggings, walking through the crocus fields. The orange stigmas are brushed from the flowers onto their leggings as they pass by. However, I now discover this to be totally untrue and obviously the product of someone's vivid imagination (not mine I hasten to add!). In fact, each bloom is handpicked and the three stigmas laboriously and carefully removed before being put to dry.

It is difficult to say exactly how much saffron to use as I have never counted the individual strands. I think 15–20 would be sufficient in most cases, and in my own recipes, I describe this as 'a good pinch'.

Serves 4

275 ml (½ pint) milk
a pinch of saffron strands
2 Florence fennel bulbs, trimmed and sliced
15 g (½ oz) butter
1 tablespoon sunflower oil

25 g (1 oz) unbleached white flour
3-4 tablespoons fresh wholewheat breadcrumbs
salt, pepper
2 tablespoons grated Parmesan cheese

Put the milk in a saucepan with the saffron, and bring to the boil. Remove from the heat, and leave to stand for 15 minutes. Strain, then discard the saffron strands.

Place the fennel in a pan with a small amount of water. Simmer until barely tender. Drain but reserve the cooking liquid. Arrange the fennel in the base of a gratin dish.

Heat together the butter and oil in a pan, and stir in the flour. Cook for a minute or two until the mixture bubbles, then remove from the heat. Gradually add the saffron milk, stirring well after each addition. Return to the heat, and bring to the boil. Simmer gently until the sauce begins to thicken. Thin down with the cooking liquid until the sauce is of a pouring consistency. Pour this over the fennel. Season the breadcrumbs before scattering them over the dish. Sprinkle the Parmesan cheese on top, and put under a hot grill to brown. Serve immediately.

BAKED TOMATOES WITH CHIVES

Serves 4–6

4–6 tomatoes, halved
1–2 tablespoons olive oil

2–3 tablespoons chopped
fresh chives

Place the tomatoes on a lightly oiled baking tray. Brush with olive oil, and sprinkle the chives over the top. Bake in a preheated oven, gas mark 5 (190°C/375°F), for 15 minutes until tender.

ORIENTAL RICE SALAD

Serves 4–6

225 g (8 oz) long grain
brown rice
a scant 575 ml (1 pint) water
100 g (4 oz) frozen peas
100 g (4 oz) button
mushrooms, sliced
1 yellow pepper, diced
50–75 g (2–3 oz) redskin
peanuts

25 g (1 oz) raisins
1 clove of garlic, peeled and
crushed
2.5 cm (1 inch) fresh root
ginger, peeled and grated
2 tablespoons sesame oil
2 tablespoons shoyu soya
sauce

Put the rice and water in a pan, and bring to the boil. Cover and simmer for 30 minutes without stirring. Put the peas on top of the rice, and cook for a further 5–8 minutes until all the water has been absorbed and the rice is dry and tender. Mix in the mushrooms, pepper, peanuts, raisins, garlic and ginger. Mix together the oil and soya sauce, then pour this over the salad. Carefully stir together all the ingredients. Spoon into a large shallow dish or on to a baking tray, and spread the rice out fairly thinly. Leave to cool. Transfer to an attractive serving dish before taking to the table.

SADDLEBACK POTATOES

Scrub the potatoes. Cut each one as if into slices but do not cut right through. Brush with oil, and bake as for jacket potatoes in a moderate to hot oven for 1–1½ hours.

POMMES DAUPHINOIS

Serves 4-6

675 g (1½ lb) potatoes, sliced
20 g (¾ oz) unbleached
   white flour

275 ml (½ pint) milk
freshly ground black pepper

Put a layer of potatoes in the base of an ovenproof dish, and sprinkle with flour. Repeat the layers until all the potatoes are used up. Season the milk with black pepper, and pour this over the potatoes. Bake in a preheated oven, gas mark 6 (200°C/400°F), for 1 hour until soft.

SCALLOPED POTATOES AND ROSEMARY

Serves 4

450 g (1 lb) potatoes, thinly
   sliced
1 onion, thinly sliced
3-4 sprigs of fresh rosemary

150 ml (¼ pint) water
2 teaspoons tomato purée
salt, pepper

Arrange the potatoes and onion in alternative layers in an ovenproof casserole, and place a sprig of rosemary on top of each layer. Mix together the water and tomate purée until well blended, and season to taste. Pour this over the potatoes, and bake in a preheated oven, gas mark 7 (220°C/425°F), for 50-60 minutes until soft and lightly browned on top.

Main Course Dishes

GOLDEN NUTTY CRUMBLE

Serves 4

FOR THE CRUMBLE
75 g (3 oz) ground peanuts
50 g (2 oz) mature Cheddar
cheese, grated
75 g (3 oz) fresh wholewheat
breadcrumbs
½ level teaspoon dried basil
½ level teaspoon dried
oregano
1 level teaspoon ready-made
English mustard
2 tablespoons sunflower oil

FOR THE FILLING
2 carrots, sliced
1 stick of celery, chopped

275 ml (½ pint) milk
1 bay leaf
100 g (4 oz) frozen peas
100 g (4 oz) button
mushrooms, sliced
2 small courgettes, sliced
1 tablespoon chopped fresh
parsley
25 g (1 oz) butter
25 g (1 oz) wholewheat flour
2 tablespoons natural
yoghurt
2 eggs
salt, pepper

To make the crumble mixture, put the ground peanuts, grated cheese, breadcrumbs and dried herbs in a bowl, and mix together well. Rub in the mustard and oil with the fingertips. Press into the base of a shallow 20 cm (8 inch) ovenproof dish, or loose-bottomed cake tin, and bake in a preheated oven, gas mark 6 (200°C/400°F), for 10–12 minutes until lightly coloured.

Meanwhile, put the carrots, celery, milk and bay leaf in a pan. Bring to the boil, cover and simmer for 8–10 minutes. Add the peas, mushrooms, courgettes and parsley, and continue to cook until the vegetables are barely tender. Drain well but reserve the flavoured milk and the cooked vegetables. Remove the bay leaf.

Melt the butter in a clean pan, and stir in the flour. Cook for a minute or two until the mixture bubbles. Remove from the heat, then gradually add the reserved milk, stirring well after each addition. Stir in the cooked vegetables, and return to the heat. Bring to the boil, stirring well. Once again remove from the heat. Leave to cool for a minute or two. Beat together the yoghurt and eggs before stirring into the vegetable sauce. Season to taste.

Spoon the mixture over the crumble base, and return to the oven. Bake for a further 20–25 minutes until firm to the touch. Serve with jacket potatoes and a green vegetable.

LENTIL AND VEGETABLE PIE

A delicious vegetable pie which will appeal to vegetarians and non-vegetarians alike. It uses two types of lentils, green ones and the much smaller and darker *Puy* lentils. *Puy* lentils are charcoal coloured, with perhaps a hint of green, and are named after the old volcanic region of that name in central France. If Puy lentils are not available, use the slightly larger continental lentil.

Serves 4

FOR THE FILLING
50 g (2 oz) green lentils
50 g (2 oz) *Puy* lentils
6 whole cloves
1 onion, peeled
1 bay leaf
275 ml (½ pint) water
1 tablespoon olive oil
225 g (8 oz) leeks, thinly sliced
100 g (4 oz) button mushrooms, thinly sliced
1 tablespoon chopped fresh parsley
2 teaspoons chopped fresh mint

2 tablespoons shoyu soya sauce
freshly ground black pepper

FOR THE PASTRY
275 g (10 oz) wholewheat self-raising flour
100 g (4 oz) firm butter, grated
2 tablespoons sunflower oil
3–4 tablespoons cold water

FOR THE GLAZE
a little beaten egg *or* milk

To make the filling, sort through the lentils and remove any small stones or pieces of grit. Push the cloves into the whole onion, and place in a pan with the bay leaf, lentils and water. Simmer for 50-60 minutes, adding more water if necessary, or pressure-cook at *high* pressure for 10-12 minutes until the lentils are soft. Drain and remove the bay leaf and cloves. Finely chop the onion.

Heat the oil in a frying pan, and sauté the leeks and mushrooms until they begin to soften. Add the lentil and onion mixture, the chopped parsley and mint and the soya sauce. Season to taste with black pepper. Cook the mixture gently, stirring frequently, until it is fairly dry. Leave to cool.

Meanwhile, make the pastry. Put the flour in a mixing bowl, and stir in the butter and oil with a fork. Add sufficient water to form a dough, and roll out on a lightly floured board to an oblong measuring approximately 20 × 40 cm (8 × 16 inches). Place on an oiled and lightly floured baking tray.

Spoon the filling mixture over the pastry, leaving a 2.5 cm (1 inch) gap along one of the longer sides. Roll up like a Swiss roll until only the uncovered pastry edge remains visible. Dampen this with water, then roll up completely so that the edge is underneath. Make a series of cuts in the top of the roll about 5 cm (2 inches) apart. Brush with beaten egg or milk and bake in a preheated oven, gas mark 6 (200°C/400°F), for 30–35 minutes, until golden-brown. Serve with Pommes Dauphinois (see page 74) and a colourful vegetable dish.

MOROCCAN COUSCOUS WITH CHICK-PEAS

To avoid confusion, it must be explained that couscous is the name given both to a product made from semolina, and to a delicious stew popular in North Africa. I first ate couscous at a market café in the old quarter of Marrakesh, surrounded by Bedouin Arabs and dark-skinned Moroccans. Everyone seemed to be eating the rich, highly spiced stew made from vegetables, chick-peas and mutton which was served with a veritable mountain of light fluffy grains. This version is light and none the worse for the omission of the mutton.

Couscous, the grain, is becoming increasingly popular as it cooks quickly and is light and easy to digest. Traditionally, couscous was soaked and then cooked in a sort of steamer known as a couscousier set over a pan of simmering broth or stew. However, I find that this tends to make the couscous heavy, as the grains stick together, and I generally

Saturday Evening

soak the grains in boiling water before drying them off under a moderately hot grill or in the oven. Although rather unorthodox, the results are excellent, each grain remaining light, fluffy and dry.

Serves 4

100 g (4 oz) chick-peas, soaked overnight and then drained
1 onion, chopped
1 clove of garlic, peeled and crushed
100 g (4 oz) white turnip, chopped
100 g (4 oz) swede, chopped
175 g (6 oz) shelled peas
1 stick of celery, chopped
225 g (8 oz) ripe tomatoes, chopped
2 courgettes, chopped
50 g (2 oz) raisins

a good pinch of saffron strands
425 ml (¾ pint) water
1 level teaspoon ground cumin
1 level teaspoon ground coriander
1 tablespoon chopped fresh mint
1 tablespoon chopped fresh parsley
salt, pepper
225 g (8 oz) couscous
a scant 575 ml (1 pint) boiling water

Put the chick-peas, vegetables, raisins, saffron and water in a large pan or pressure cooker. Cover and simmer for 1½–1¾ hours, adding a little more water if necessary, or pressure-cook at *high* pressure for 20 minutes. When the chick-peas are tender, uncover and cook gently for a further 3–5 minutes, stirring well to thicken the stock. Add the cumin, coriander, mint and parsley, and season to taste.

Meanwhile, put the couscous in a bowl and pour over the boiling water. Leave to stand for 15–20 minutes. Drain if necessary. Spread out on a clean cloth and roll up like a Swiss roll. Squeeze so that any surplus moisture is absorbed by the cloth. Spoon the couscous on to a large baking tray, spread thinly and place under a moderate grill or in a hot oven. Heat for several minutes, turning frequently until the couscous is dry, soft and fluffy. Serve with the vegetable stew.

STUFFED AUBERGINES WITH HERBS

Serves 3–4

3–4 aubergines
50 g (2 oz) chick–peas,
  soaked overnight and then
  drained
425 ml (¾ pint) water
100 g (4 oz) brown lentils
2 onions, finely chopped
2 cloves of garlic, peeled and
  crushed
1 tablespoon tomato purée
1 tablespoon ground
  coriander

2 teaspoons dried marjoram
½ teaspoon ground allspice
½ teaspoon dried mixed
  herbs
½–1 tablespoon shoyu soya
  sauce
2–3 tablespoons chopped
  fresh parsley
salt, pepper

FOR THE TOPPING
5 tablespoons natural
  yoghurt
½ beaten egg

Bake the aubergines in a preheated oven, gas mark 6 (200°C/400°F), for 30–35 minutes until soft. Leave to cool.

Put the chick-peas in a pan with the water, and simmer for 1 hour, or pressure-cook at *high* pressure for 15 minutes. Drain well, reserving both the stock and chick-peas. Sort through the lentils and remove any small stones or pieces of grit. Put with the chick-peas into the pan, and pour 350 ml (12 fl oz) of the reserved stock over them. Add all the remaining ingredients *except* for the soya sauce, parsley and seasoning. Cook for 50–60 minutes, adding a little more water if necessary, or pressure-cook at *high* pressure for 13–14 minutes. Drain if necessary.

Carefully cut the aubergines in half, from top to bottom, and scoop out the fleshy inside, taking care not to cut through the skins. Mash the pulpy flesh and stir into the pulse mixture. Add the soya sauce and parsley, and season to taste. Spoon the mixture into the hollow aubergine skins, and arrange in the base of a lightly oiled ovenproof dish.

To make the topping, beat together the yoghurt and egg, and then dribble a little over the top of each aubergine half.

Return the aubergines to the oven, and bake for 25–30 minutes until heated through. Serve with brown rice or pitta bread and Courgette and Tomato Agrodolce (see page 71).

FISH PIE SUPREME

A fish pie with a difference – the hint of orange in the sauce adds piquancy and also helps to counteract the richness of the crab meat.

Serves 4

FOR THE FILLING
**425 ml (¾ pint) fish stock
(see page 155)
350 g (12 oz) monkfish
100 g (4 oz) peeled prawns
100 g (4 oz) crab meat
(white and brown meat)
50 g (2 oz) butter
50 g (2 oz) unbleached white
flour
grated rind of 1 orange
2 tablespoons chopped fresh
chives**

**¼–½ level teaspoon Cayenne
pepper
salt, pepper**

FOR THE PASTRY
**175 g (6 oz) wholewheat
flour
1 level teaspoon baking
powder
75 g (3 oz) butter, diced
6 teaspoons cold water**

FOR THE GLAZE
a little beaten egg *or* milk

Put the fish stock into a pan, and bring to the boil. Reduce the heat and, when barely simmering, add the monkfish, and poach for 6–8 minutes until tender. Lift from the pan and reserve the stock. When cool enough to handle, chop the fish into bite-sized pieces, discarding any bones. Put the cooked fish into a bowl with the prawns and crab meat. Set aside until needed.

Melt the butter in a clean pan, and stir in the flour. Cook for a minute or two until the mixture bubbles. Remove from the heat, then gradually add 375-400 ml (13–14 fl oz) of the fish stock, stirring well after each addition. Return to the heat and bring to the boil, stirring frequently, until the sauce thickens. Pour this over the fish, then add the grated orange rind, the chives and Cayenne pepper. Season to taste, and mix together carefully. Spoon into a pie dish or four individual, ovenproof dishes – don't overfill the containers. Leave to cool.

To make the pastry, put the flour in a mixing bowl with the baking powder, and mix together. Rub in the butter with the fingertips until the mixture resembles breadcrumbs. Add the water, and mix to form a pastry dough. Roll out on a lightly floured board to 0.6 cm (¼ inch) thickness, and use to cover the pie filling. Trim the pastry edges, brush with beaten egg or milk, and make a slit in the top. Bake in a preheated oven, gas mark 6 (200°C/400°F), for 25 minutes until lightly browned. Serve with Saddleback Potatoes.

MEDITERRANEAN LASAGNE

Serves 4–6

1 tablespoon olive oil
225 g (8 oz) wholewheat
  lasagne

FOR THE MUSHROOM SAUCE
2 tablespoons olive oil
225 g (8 oz) button
  mushrooms, sliced
1 level tablespoon
  unbleached white flour
150 ml (¼ pint) natural
  yoghurt
freshly grated nutmeg

FOR THE FISH SAUCE
425 ml (¾ pint) fish stock
  (see page 155)
450 g (1 lb) halibut fillets,
  skinned
50 g (2 oz) butter
50 g (2 oz) unbleached white
  flour
a scant 150 ml (¼ pint) milk
100 g (4 oz) peeled prawns
1–2 tablespoons chopped
  fresh parsley
salt, pepper
olive oil as required

Fill a large pan with boiling water, add the oil and lasagne, and cook briskly for 10–12 minutes until *al dente*. Drain well.

To make the mushroom sauce, heat the oil in a saucepan, and sauté the mushrooms for 4–5 minutes. Stir in the flour, and cook for 1–2 minutes until the mixture bubbles. Add the yoghurt, and mix together well. Season to taste with nutmeg. Remove from the heat.

To make the fish sauce, put the fish stock into a clean pan, bring to a slow boil, then reduce the heat until the surface of the stock is merely quivering. Add the fish, and poach for 4–6 minutes until barely tender. Drain well, and reserve the stock. When cool enough to handle, chop the halibut into bite-sized pieces, removing any bones. Melt the butter in the pan, and stir in the flour. Cook for a minute or two until the mixture bubbles. Remove from the heat, then gradually add the stock and milk, stirring well after each addition. Return to the heat and bring to the boil, stirring all the time, until the sauce thickens. Add the cooked halibut, the prawns and parsley. Season to taste.

Brush a large ovenproof dish with olive oil. Put a layer of cooked lasagne in the base. Pour over half the fish sauce. Cover with another layer of lasagne and then the mushroom sauce. Top with the remaining lasagne and the fish sauce. Bake in a preheated oven, gas mark 6 (200°C/400°F), for 20–25 minutes until heated through. Cool slightly before serving with a tossed salad.

SALMON TROUT EN PAPILLOTE WITH BEURRE BLANC SAUCE

I make no apologies for the fact that this recipe first appeared in another of my books, *The New Fish Cookbook* (Piatkus 1986), for salmon trout is one of my favourite fish. It has been described as 'the perfect fish', combining, as it does, the very best of the trout and salmon. Small salmon trout can be treated as if they were trout and larger ones as if they were salmon. They can be cooked whole or in steaks and are excellent poached, grilled, baked or, as in the following recipe, cooked *en papillote* – baked in a paper parcel, with a sprig of fresh herb and a knob of butter. Accompaniments should be kept light in flavour and texture so that the excellence of the fish can speak for itself.

Serves 4

4 salmon trout steaks
15 g (½ oz) melted butter
salt, pepper
4 sprigs of fresh parsley
4 slices of lemon

FOR THE SAUCE
juice of ½ lemon
1 tablespoon white wine
  vinegar
1 shallot, finely chopped
50 g (2 oz) unsalted butter

Cut four sheets of greaseproof paper so that each is large enough to wrap around one of the salmon trout steaks. Brush the paper with melted butter, and place a salmon trout steak in the centre of each. Lightly season, then lay a sprig of parsley and a slice of lemon on top. Fold the paper over the fish, tucking the ends underneath to form a loose but secure parcel. Place on a baking tray, and bake in a preheated oven, gas mark 6 (200°C/400°F), for 15–20 minutes until tender.

Put the lemon juice, wine vinegar and the shallot in a small pan, and bring to the boil. Boil briskly until the liquid is reduced to a scant tablespoon. Strain, then return to a clean pan, set over a low heat, and gradually stir in the butter, a knob at at time, beating well as more and more butter is added. When the butter has been used up, the sauce should resemble shiny whipped cream.

When the salmon trout is cooked, unwrap each parcel, taking care not to spill the cooking juices. Lay the fish on warm plates, and pour over the cooking juices. Put the sauce in a small bowl or sauce-boat, and serve with the fish, together with new potatoes and green beans.

BRANDIED CHICKEN

Serves 4-6

1 oven-ready chicken,
 weighing 1.5 kg (3 lb)

FOR THE STOCK
575 ml (1 pint) water
1 slice of onion
1 stick of celery, chopped
½ carrot, sliced
1 bay leaf
6 black peppercorns
1 sprig of fresh parsley
1 sprig of fresh thyme

FOR THE REMAINING INGREDIENTS
40 g (1½ oz) butter
1 tablespoon olive oil
1 clove of garlic, peeled and
 crushed
1 onion, finely chopped
25 g (1 oz) unbleached white
 flour
2 tablespoons brandy
freshly grated nutmeg
salt, pepper
100 g (4 oz) peeled prawns

Joint the chicken. Remove the skin and any visible fat from the 6 pieces. Put the wings and giblets into a pan, then add all the stock ingredients. Bring to the boil, cover and simmer gently for 30 minutes. Strain and reserve the stock.

Heat together the butter and oil in a large, heavy, casserole-type pan, and sauté the chicken pieces for 5–7 minutes, turning occasionally until lightly browned. Remove with a slotted spoon, and keep aside until needed. Add the garlic and onion, and sauté until soft and golden. Stir in the flour and let the mixture bubble. Remove from the heat, then gradually add 425 ml (¾ pint) of the reserved chicken stock, a little at a time, stirring well after each addition. Return to the heat and bring to the boil, stirring all the time, until the sauce thickens.

Return the chicken pieces to the pan. Flame the brandy in a warm ladle, and pour this over the chicken. Season with nutmeg and black pepper. Cover and simmer for 25–35 minutes until tender. Stir in the prawns 5 minutes before serving, then heat through and season to taste. Serve with brown rice and a green salad.

CHICKEN WITH ORANGE AND SAFFRON SAUCE

Serves 4–6

1 oven-ready chicken,
  weighing 1.5 kg (3 lb)
425 ml (¾ pint) chicken
  stock (see page 156)
1–2 tablespoons sunflower
  oil
1 onion, finely chopped

2 good pinches of saffron
  strands
grated rind of 1 orange
350 ml (12 fl oz) natural
  yoghurt
1 egg
1 heaped tablespoon
  unbleached white flour
freshly ground black pepper

Joint the chicken. Remove the skin and any visible fat from the 6 pieces. Use the wings and giblets to make the stock as described on page 156.

Heat the oil in a large, heavy, casserole-type pan, and sauté the onion for 5–7 minutes until soft and golden. Gradually stir in the chicken stock, and then the saffron. Add the chicken pieces, cover and bring to the boil. Simmer for 20 minutes. Sprinkle the grated orange rind over the top, and cook for a further 5 minutes.

Mix together thoroughly the yoghurt, egg and flour. Stir a ladle of hot stock from the pan into the mixture, and then pour the whole lot over the chicken. Mix together carefully. Cover the pan and continue cooking for 5–10 minutes until the chicken is tender and the sauce heated through. Season with black pepper before serving. Serve with new potatoes and a green vegetable.

NORTH COUNTRY RABBIT PIE

There are no rabbit bones to worry about in this dish.

Serves 4

1 oven-ready rabbit, jointed

FOR THE STOCK
1 bay leaf
½ carrot, sliced
1 slice of onion
1 sprig of fresh parsley
6 black peppercorns

FOR THE REMAINING INGREDIENTS
wholewheat flour for dusting
2–3 tablespoons sunflower
  oil
1 onion, chopped
100 g (4 oz) lean, unsmoked
  bacon, trimmed and
  chopped

2 tablespoons dry sherry
2 slices of lemon
1 bay leaf
½ teaspoon dried marjoram
½ teaspoon dried oregano
1 large carrot, chopped
75 g (3 oz) celeriac, chopped
freshly ground black pepper

FOR THE PASTRY
175 g (6 oz) wholewheat
  flour
75 g (3 oz) butter, diced
6 teaspoons water
milk to glaze

To make the stock, put the rabbit's rib cage and backbone, liver, heart and kidneys into a pan with the bay leaf, carrot, onion, parsley and black peppercorns. Barely cover with cold water and bring to the boil. Cover and simmer gently for 30 minutes. Drain well and discard the solids.

Dust the remaining rabbit pieces with flour. Heat the oil in a heavy, casserole-type pan, and brown the rabbit on all sides. Remove with a slotted spoon and keep aside. Put the onion and bacon into the pan, and sauté for 4–5 minutes. Return the rabbit to the pan and pour the stock over. Add the dry sherry, slices of lemon, bay leaf, marjoram and oregano. Cover and simmer gently for 45 minutes to 1 hour until the rabbit is tender. Once again, remove the rabbit with a slotted spoon and leave aside to cool slightly. If necessary, boil the remaining stock briskly until reduced to approximately 275 ml (½ pint). Discard the bay leaf and lemon slices.

When cool enough to handle, remove the meat from the rabbit bones and place on the base of a pie dish. Pour over the stock. Cook the carrot and celeriac in a small pan of water until barely tender, drain and then mix with the rabbit. Season to taste with black pepper.

To make the pastry, put the flour in a mixing bowl and rub in the butter, with the fingertips, until the mixture resembles breadcrumbs.

Add the water, and knead to form a pastry dough. Roll out on a lightly floured board to 0.6 cm (¼ inch) thickness and use to cover the pie filling. Trim the pastry edges, and press to seal. Brush the top with milk, and make two or three slits in the top to allow the steam to escape. Bake in a preheated oven, gas mark 6 (200°C/400°F), for 25 minutes. Serve with savoy cabbage and jacket potatoes.

BLANQUETTE OF RABBIT

Rabbit is generally underrated as a meat and deserves more attention. It is flavoursome and good value, and this method of preparation overcomes the problems associated with it having small bones. Given some notice, most butchers will be happy to skin and bone it for you.

Serves 4

1 oven-ready rabbit, jointed	350 g (12 oz) button onions,
½ onion, chopped	halved if necessary
1 carrot, chopped	275 ml (½ pint) milk
2 bay leaves	1 sprig of fresh tarragon
2 sprigs of fresh parsley	1 sprig of fresh savory
10 black peppercorns	25 g (1 oz) butter
425 ml (¾ pint) water	25 g (1 oz) unbleached white
2-3 tablespoons sunflower	flour
oil	salt, pepper

Trim the meat from the rabbit's rib cage and backbone, and put to one side. Put the trimmed bones, the rabbit's liver, heart and kidneys in a small pan with the chopped onion, carrot, 1 bay leaf, 1 sprig of parsley, the peppercorns and water. Bring to the boil, cover and simmer for 25 minutes. Strain and reserve the stock.

Heat the oil in a heavy-based pan, and sauté the button onions until they begin to brown. Remove from the pan with a slotted spoon, and keep aside. Add the rabbit joints and trimmed meat, and brown on all sides. Return the onions to the pan, and pour 275 ml (½ pint) reserved rabbit stock and the milk over the meat. Add the remaining herbs, bring to the boil, cover with a tight-fitting lid, and simmer gently for 1–1½ hours until the rabbit is tender.

Pour the contents of the pan into a sieve, and discard the herbs. Reserve both the stock and solids. When cool enough to handle, remove the meat from the bones, and put into a shallow, ovenproof dish with the cooked onions.

Melt the butter in a small pan, stir in the flour, and let the mixture bubble. Remove from the heat, then gradually add 425 ml (¾ pint) of the reserved stock, stirring well after each addition. Return to the heat and bring to the boil, stirring all the time, until the sauce thickens.

Pour the sauce over the rabbit and onions, and gently mix together. Season to taste. Put under a hot grill, and heat until the sauce is bubbling and beginning to brown on top. Serve with new potatoes or brown rice, and follow with a crisp, refreshing salad.

BRAISED PEPPER STEAK

Serves 4–6

4–6 braising steaks, each weighing about 100 g (4 oz)
1 tablespoon black peppercorns, crushed
2–3 tablespoons sunflower oil
275 ml (½ pint) dry white wine

275 ml (½ pint) beef stock (see page 156)
1 clove of garlic, peeled and crushed
1 large onion, chopped

Tenderize the meat with a meat tenderizer or a rolling-pin. Spread the crushed peppercorns, a few at a time, on a board or plate, and press the steaks on to them. Shake off any surplus. Do not be too liberal with the crushed peppercorns as they are hot.

Heat the oil in a casserole-type pan, and brown the steaks on both sides. Pour the wine and beef stock over, then add the garlic and onion. Cover and cook in a preheated oven, gas mark 6 (200°C/400°F), for 1-1¼ hours until the meat is tender. Serve with Scalloped Potatoes and Rosemary (page 74), Baked Tomatoes with Chives (see page 73) and a bowl of watercress.

HALF AND HALF MOUSSAKA

A moussaka made with a mixture of meat and lentils. It is an admirable way of reducing the fat intake while increasing the fibre content of one's diet. The combination of minced beef and brown lentils can also be used to make bolognese sauces, shepherd's pies, burgers and the like. Some people use aduki beans in preference to brown lentils.

Serves 4

100 g (4 oz) brown lentils
1 bay leaf
275 ml (½ pint) water
1–2 tablespoons olive oil
1 large onion, chopped
1 clove of garlic, peeled and crushed
225 g (8 oz) lean minced beef *or* lamb
450 g (1 lb) ripe tomatoes, chopped
150 ml (¼ pint) red wine
1 tablespoon tomato purée (optional)
½–1 teaspoon mixed dried herbs

½ teaspoon dried oregano
salt, pepper
2 aubergines, thinly sliced

FOR THE TOPPING
15 g (½ oz) butter
1 tablespoon olive oil
25 g (1 oz) unbleached white flour
425 ml (¾ pint) milk
freshly grated nutmeg
50 g (2 oz) Cheddar cheese, grated
1 tablespoon grated Parmesan cheese

Sort through the lentils and remove any small stones and pieces of grit. Put into a large pan or pressure cooker with the bay leaf. Pour over the water, cover and bring to the boil. Simmer for 50–60 minutes, adding a little more water if necessary, or pressure-cook at *high* pressure for 12–13 minutes. When cooked, the lentils should be soft and fairly dry. Drain, if necessary, and remove the bay leaf.

Heat the oil in a large pan, and sauté the onion and garlic for 5–7 minutes until soft and golden. Stir in the meat, and cook gently until lightly browned. Add the tomatoes, red wine, tomato purée (if using it) and the cooked lentils. Add the dried herbs, and season to taste. Cover and simmer gently for 20–30 minutes until the meat is tender and the sauce thick and richly flavoured. Spoon into an ovenproof dish.

Heat a large, heavy frying pan, and dry fry the aubergine slices until lightly browned and slightly soft. Arrange on top of the filling mixture.

To make the topping, heat the butter and oil in a pan, stir in the flour and let the mixture bubble. Remove from the heat, then gradually add the milk, stirring well after each addition. Return to the heat and bring to the boil, stirring all the time until the sauce thickens. Season with a little freshly grated nutmeg, then stir in the cheeses.

Pour the sauce over the aubergines, then bake in a preheated oven, gas mark 6 (200°C/400°F), for 20 minutes until the sauce is bubbling and the filling heated through. Serve with crusty granary bread and a salad.

CARBONADE OF BEEF

A full-bodied beef stew.

Serves 4–6

675 g (1½ lb) silverside of
  beef, cut into strips 1.25
  cm (½ inch) thick and
  2.5–5 cm (1–2 inches)
  long
575 ml (1 pint) bitter beer
2–3 tablespoons sunflower
  oil
2 onions, chopped

40 g (1½ oz) wholewheat
  flour
1 bay leaf
1 tablespoon chopped fresh
  parsley
1 tablespoon chopped fresh
  thyme
1 teaspoon ready-made
  English mustard
salt, pepper

Put the meat into a bowl, and pour over the beer. Cover and leave in a cool place to marinate for 2–3 hours. Drain well, and reserve both the meat and marinade.

Heat half the oil in a casserole-type pan, and sauté the onions for 3–4 minutes. Lift from the pan with a slotted spoon, and set aside until needed. Toss the meat in the flour, shake off any surplus and then brown in the pan in the remaining oil. Pour the marinade over, a little at a time, stirring well after each addition. Return the onions to the pan, then add the bay leaf, parsley and thyme. The marinade should just cover the ingredients; add more beef stock or water if necessary. Cover and place in a preheated oven, gas mark 3 (160°C/325°F), for 2¼–2½ hours until the meat is tender. Stir in the mustard, and season to taste. Serve with Pommes Dauphinois (see page 74) and a selection of vegetables.

Saturday Evening

PAPRIKA PORK

Serves 4

1–2 tablespoons sunflower
   oil
2 onions, chopped
550 g (1¼ lb) lean pork,
   chopped
2 cloves of garlic, peeled and
   crushed
1 tablespoon paprika
¼ teaspoon chilli powder

1 tablespoon unbleached
   white flour
275 ml (½ pint) chicken
   stock (see page 156)
1 green pepper, chopped
3 ripe tomatoes, chopped
1 tablespoon tomato purée
150 ml (¼ pint) natural
   yoghurt
salt, pepper

Heat the oil in a heavy-based, casserole-type pan, and sauté the onions for 4–5 minutes. Add the meat, and brown on all sides. Stir in the garlic, paprika and chilli powder, and cook for 1–2 minutes, making sure that the spices do not catch on the bottom of the pan. Add the flour, and continue to cook, stirring frequently, for 1–2 minutes. Stir in the stock, a little at a time, then add the green pepper, tomatoes and tomato purée. Cover with a tight-fitting lid, and simmer gently for 1¼–1½ hours, stirring occasionally, until the meat is tender. Pour the yoghurt into a small bowl or measuring jug, and add some of the stock from the stew. Mix together well. Remove the stew from the heat before stirring in the yoghurt mixture. Season to taste. Heat through gently, taking care not to boil. Serve with sautéed potatoes and Stir-fried Carrot and Celeriac (see page 70).

LASAGNE CORDON VERT

A moist, flavoursome vegetarian lasagne that is very easy to make.

Serves 4

FOR THE SAUCE
450 g (1 lb) ripe tomatoes
3 tablespoons water
½ teaspoon mixed dried herbs
½ tablespoon tomato purée, optional
salt, pepper

FOR THE REMAINING INGREDIENTS
2-3 tablespoons olive oil
175 g (6 oz) wholewheat lasagne
1 onion, finely chopped
1 clove of garlic, peeled and crushed

175 g (6 oz) button mushrooms, sliced
175 g (6 oz) redskin peanuts, ground
50 g (2 oz) soft wholewheat breadcrumbs
1 tablespoon shoyu soya sauce
freshly ground black pepper
225 g (8 oz) low fat cream cheese
2 tablespoons natural yoghurt
25-50 g (1-2 oz) mature Cheddar cheese, grated

Chop the tomatoes finely and put into a pan with the water and mixed dried herbs. Cover and cook gently for 10–15 minutes until very soft. If necessary, remove the lid and boil briskly to drive off excess water. Pass the tomato mixture through the fine blade of a vegetable mouli or blend in a liquidizer or food processor until smooth. Enrich with tomato purée, if using it, and season to taste with black pepper. Keep aside until needed.

Fill a large pan with boiling water, add 1 tablespoon of the oil and the lasagne and cook briskly for 10–12 minutes until *al dente*. Drain well.

Heat the remaining oil in a frying pan, and sauté the onion and garlic for 5–7 minutes until soft and golden. Stir in the mushrooms, and cook for several minutes more. Remove from the heat, and add the ground peanuts, breadcrumbs and soya sauce. Season to taste with black pepper. Blend together the cream cheese and yoghurt in a liquidizer or food processor or mix in a small bowl.

Brush a large, ovenproof dish with olive oil. Put half the cooked lasagne in the base. Spoon over half the cream cheese mixture followed by half the nutty mixture and finally half the tomato sauce. Repeat the layers using up the remaining ingredients. Sprinkle the grated cheese on top and bake in a preheated oven, gas mark 6 (200°C/400°F), for 25 minutes until heated through. Serve with a side salad.

Puddings and Desserts

BLACKBERRY AND APPLE CRUMBLE

Serves 4–6

350 g (12 oz) eating apples,
  peeled, cored and sliced
350 g (12 oz) blackberries
2–3 tablespoons
  concentrated apple juice

FOR THE CRUMBLE
100 g (4 oz) porridge oats
75 g (3 oz) wholewheat flour

25 g (1 oz) desiccated
  coconut
5 tablespoons sunflower oil
1 tablespoon concentrated
  apple juice
a few drops of vanilla essence

Cook the apples in the minimum of water (barely cover the bottom of the pan) until they begin to soften. Stir in the blackberries, and place in a pie dish. Dribble the concentrated apple juice over the top to taste – the amount needed will depend to a large extent on the sweetness of the blackberries.

To make the crumble, mix together all the dry ingredients in a bowl. Rub in the oil, concentrated apple juice and vanilla essence.

Sprinkle the crumble mixture over the fruit, and press down lightly with the fingertips. Bake in a preheated oven, gas mark 5 (190°C/375°F), for 25–30 minutes until golden-brown.

LEMON PUDDING

Many recipes call for the grated rind (or zest) of the lemon which contains the aromatic oils and, therefore, has a stronger flavour than the juice. Unfortunately, the growers don't seem to appreciate this fact for, more often than not, the fruit is picked unripe and then artificially ripened with ethylene gas. Some lemons are even dyed, sprayed and waxed so that they all look equally attractive. Scrubbing in warm water may remove some of these chemicals but many people prefer not to use the zest at all. When buying lemons, pick out the largest and heaviest fruits.

Serves 4

225 ml (8 fl oz) milk
2 tablespoons clear honey
2 large eggs, separated
25 g (1 oz) wholewheat
   self-raising flour

15 g (½ oz) butter, diced
juice and grated rind of 1
   lemon

Heat together the milk and honey in a small pan until well mixed. Leave aside to cool, then stir in the yolks.

   Place the flour in a small bowl, and rub in the butter until the mixture resembles breadcrumbs. Stir in the egg mixture and the juice and grated rind of the lemon. Beat the egg whites until stiff, then fold into the mixture. Pour it into an oiled pie dish, and stand it in a deep baking tray filled with warm water. Bake in a preheated oven, gas mark 4 (180°C/350°F), for 40–45 minutes until firm to the touch. Serve as soon as possible.

CARIBBEAN FRUIT SALAD

A delicious 'hot' fruit salad, ideal for a winter's evening.

Serves 4–6

1 pineapple, sliced
4 bananas, sliced
6 tablespoons fresh orange
  juice

2 tablespoons brandy
½ level teaspoon ground
  cinnamon
50 g (2 oz) desiccated
  coconut

Arrange half the pineapple in the base of an ovenproof dish. Lay the bananas on top, and cover with the remaining pineapple. Mix together the orange juice, brandy and cinnamon, and pour this over the fruit. Sprinkle the coconut on top. Bake in a preheated oven, gas mark 5 (190°C/375°F), for 25–30 minutes until the fruit begins to soften.

ORIENTAL FRUIT PLATTER WITH CASHEW NUT CREAM

The perfect solution for those of you who, like me, dislike the traditional fruit bowl brought to the table at the end of the meal. It is not that I dislike fruit – quite the contrary – I find myself torn between the different fruits, each one looking inviting and appealing. How much nicer to be able to have a taste of each kind.

Serves 4–6

1 pineapple
75 g (3 oz) seedless grapes
75 g (3 oz) lychees
1 mango
1 sweet orange *or* tangerine
1 kiwi fruit

FOR THE CASHEW NUT CREAM
100 g (4 oz) cashew nuts
125–150 ml (4–5 fl oz)
    water

Cut the pineapple in half from top to bottom, leaving the leaves attached. Scoop out the flesh, and cut into cubes. Wash the grapes and remove the stalks. Peel the lychees. Wash and thinly slice the mango. Peel the orange and cut the membrane from each segment. Peel and slice the kiwi fruit. Cut a thin slice from the bottom of one of the pineapple halves so that it can stand steady.

Fill three-quarters of each pineapple 'boat' with pineapple cubes. Starting from the leafy top, arrange a row of grapes across the partially filled pineapple, then add a row of mango slices. Follow this with a row of pineapple cubes, a row of kiwi fruit, another row of pineapple, a row of orange and finally a row of lychees. Place the halves on a flat serving plate, and pile any remaining fruit around them.

To make the cashew nut cream, blend the cashews and water in a liquidizer or food processor until smooth. Rub through a sieve for a really creamy texture. Serve with the fruit.

MARINATED STRAWBERRIES AND PEACHES

Serves 4-6

450 g (1 lb) strawberries, hulled
2 large peaches, sliced

150 ml (¼ pint) fresh orange juice

Place the strawberries in a serving dish, and mix with the peaches. Pour over the orange juice, and leave in a cool place for several hours, carefully stirring the fruit occasionally.

MIXED MELON BOWL

Mix together the flesh of a honeydew melon, an Ogen or Galia melon, and a watermelon – roughly chopped and in equal quantities. Sprinkle a little orange juice over the top, and lightly mix together. Cover and leave in a cool place to marinate for several hours. Serve in a glass bowl or the hollowed-out shell of one of the melons. Do not take to the table really cold. The flavour of the melons is best appreciated lightly chilled or at room temperature.

APRICOT MOUSSE

A light, fruity dessert that can be made several hours before it is needed.

Serves 4-6

350 g (12 oz) dried apricots
275 ml (½ pint) boiling water
2 tablespoons fresh orange juice

150 ml (¼ pint) natural yoghurt
2 egg whites
twists of orange rind

Put the apricots into a bowl, and cover with the water. Leave to soak overnight until they begin to soften.

Next day, bring the apricots to the boil, and cook gently until soft. Blend the apricots, fresh orange juice and yoghurt in a liquidizer or food processor until smooth and creamy. Whisk the egg whites until stiff and peaked, and fold into the mixture. Spoon into individual dishes, and decorate with twists of orange rind.

RASPBERRY SORBET

Sorbets are not really difficult to make, and there is no need for any special equipment other than a deep freeze compartment. The delicate flavour of fresh raspberries is enhanced by the addition of rosewater – this can be bought from most large chemists. It is difficult to give precise instructions about how much to use since concentrations vary. It is best to start with a few drops, gradually adding more, until the flavour complements rather than overwhelms that of the raspberries.

Serves 4–6

450 g (1 lb) raspberries	**juice of ½ lemon**
50 ml (2 fl oz) concentrated	**rosewater**
apple juice	**4 egg whites**

Rub the raspberries through a nylon sieve and discard the seeds. Put the fruit purée into a pan with the concentrated apple and lemon juice, and bring to the boil. Boil fairly briskly for 10 minutes, stirring frequently until reduced by about half. The mixture's reduced volume should measure approximately 150–175 ml (5-6 fl oz). Flavour to taste with rosewater, pour into a plastic box, and cover with a tight-fitting lid. Put into the freezer to firm up. Stir every hour or so to ensure even freezing. When it has frozen to a slush, remove from the freezer, and mix well.

   Whisk the egg whites until stiff and peaked, and fold into the fruit slush. When evenly mixed, return to the freezer. Place in a refrigerator 30-40 minutes before serving.

COEUR DE CRÈME WITH BLACKCURRANT PURÉE

As the name suggests, this smooth, creamy, low fat mould is shaped like a heart and is topped with a fresh fruit purée. The simplest and most attractive way of preparing it is to use white glazed *coeur à fromage* cream-cheese moulds which have perforated bases for drainage. They are readily available, in various sizes, in cookshops but are quite expensive and not particularly versatile. Nonetheless, they are well worth buying if you enjoy this type of dessert. It is, however, possible to use a sieve lined with muslin. The resultant dome-shaped mould can look attractive if served on a decorative plate with the fruit purée spooned over the top, but the effect is not as impressive as when using heart-shaped moulds.

Serves 4–6

275 g (10 oz) ripe blackcurrants	225 g (8 oz) cottage cheese
1–2 tablespoons concentrated apple juice	150 ml (¼ pint) thick set natural yoghurt
	2 egg whites

Top and tail the blackcurrants. Put 50 g (2 oz) of them in a small pan with 1-2 tablespoons concentrated apple juice. Cook gently, stirring frequently, until the mixture thickens. Leave to cool.

Rub the cheese through a sieve, then stir in the yoghurt and cooked blackcurrants. Beat the egg whites until stiff and peaked, then fold into the *crème*. Line the base of a *coeur de crème* pot with muslin, and spoon in the mixture. Stand on a plate or baking tray, and leave in a cool place to drain.

Rub the remaining blackcurrants through a sieve, and sweeten to taste with concentrated apple juice. Cover and leave overnight to thicken.

Next day, tip the *coeur de crème* from its pot, and serve with the blackcurrant purée.

TOFU CHEESECAKE

A light and flavoursome cheesecake that is low in calories.

Serves 6

FOR THE BASE
100 g (4 oz) wholewheat
  flour
100 g (4 oz) porridge oats
5 tablespoons soya oil
1 tablespoon concentrated
  apple juice

FOR THE FILLING
275 g (10 oz) Silken tofu,
  drained
2–3 tablespoons clear honey

50 g (2 oz) currants
grated rind and juice of ½
  lemon
a good pinch of mixed spice
150 ml (¼ pint) diluted
  apple juice
2 level teaspoons arrowroot
2 eggs, separated

To make the base, put the flour and porridge oats in a mixing bowl, and rub in the oil. Add the concentrated apple juice, and mix well. Press into the base of a 20 cm (8 inch) loose-bottomed sandwich tin, and bake in a preheated oven, gas mark 6 (200°C/400°F), for 10-12 minutes.

To make the filling, put the tofu and honey in a liquidizer or food processor, and blend until smooth. Spoon into a bowl, then add the currants, grated rind and juice of ½ lemon and the mixed spice. Mix together the apple juice and arrowroot, and pour into a small pan. Gradually bring to the boil, stirring continuously, until the mixture thickens. Spoon into the tofu mixture, and mix well. Add the egg yolks. Whisk the egg whites until stiff and peaked, then fold into the mixture.

Spoon the filling over the crumble base, and return to the oven. Bake for 30 minutes, then reduce the oven temperature to gas mark 4 (180°C/350°F), and cook for a further 25–30 minutes until firm to the touch and golden-brown.

YOGHURT CHEESE

Serves 6

425 ml (¾ pint) natural
  yoghurt
sesame seeds

cumin powder
fresh herbs (chives, tarragon,
  savory), finely chopped

Line a sieve with muslin, and stand it over a bowl. Pour the yoghurt into the sieve, and leave overnight to drain. Next day, place a tight-fitting lid inside the sieve and stand a 900 g (2 lb) weight on top. Leave overnight again. Keep chilled until needed.

Pound a small quantity of sesame seeds, and flavour with a good pinch or two of cumin powder. Roll half the cheese into small balls, and dust with the sesame mixture. Shape the remaining cheese into a log, and roll in the chopped herbs. Arrange on a serving plate with a selection of savoury biscuits.

SAVOURY DIGESTIVES

Makes 15 small biscuits

50 g (2 oz) wholewheat flour
50 g (2 oz) fine oatmeal
a pinch of bicarbonate of
  soda

40 g (1½ oz) butter, diced
½ beaten egg
1 teaspoon clear honey
oil as required

Mix together the dry ingredients in a bowl. Rub in the butter, then add the egg and honey. Mix together to form a dough. Roll out on a lightly floured board to 0.6 cm (¼ inch) thickness, and cut into shapes. Place on an oiled baking tray, and bake in a preheated oven, gas mark 6 (200°C/400°F), for 8–10 minutes until lightly browned.

Sunday Morning

What is generally thought of as the 'British breakfast' dates from the eighteenth century when porridge, fish, bacon, eggs, toast, marmalade and copious cups of tea began to replace the traditional meal of cold meat, pies, cheese, bread and beer. One can only hazard a guess as to the reasons for these changes but it is likely that speed and ease of preparation became major considerations in all but the wealthiest of households and that, following the Industrial Revolution, the new breed of city dwellers found the large breakfasts of their forefathers a little too substantial for their increasingly sedentary life-styles.

The trend towards lighter breakfasts has carried on unabated ever since, and, nowadays, few people take the time or trouble to prepare a cooked breakfast. Most prefer to eat cereal and toast, while some go without altogether. While I am sure that nothing I say will persuade this latter group to eat before mid morning, there is evidence to suggest that people who do not eat first thing are appreciably less efficient, less productive and noticeably less good tempered than those who do. This is because in the morning, after a seven to ten hour period without food, the body's blood sugar level is naturally low and needs replenishing before one sets about the day's business. Almost any food will provide the body with some energy but it is best to choose ones which are high in starchy carbohydrates and fibre and low in sugar. Such foods will ensure a steady supply right through until lunchtime without the need to boost supplies mid morning with a biscuit, pastry or chocolate bar.

I am the first to admit that speed and ease of preparation are key factors when choosing foods for weekday mornings, but I make a point of redressing the balance at weekends, particularly on Sundays when there is usually time to relax and enjoy a leisurely breakfast. On such occasions I like to serve muffins, croissants or brioches with wide-brimmed cups of *café au lait*. In the summer, soft fruits and yoghurt, creamy cheeses and freshly squeezed juices are delicious, while a traditional cooked breakfast of porridge or bacon and eggs makes a welcome start to a winter's morning together with lots of hot tea.

Sunday Morning

HOT FRUIT SURPRISE

Serves 4-6

100 g (4 oz) prunes
100 g (4 oz) dried apricots
575 ml (1 pint) water
50 g (2 oz) raisins *or* sultanas
100 g (4 oz) seedless grapes
2 bananas, sliced

275 ml (½ pint) unsweetened
    orange and apricot juice,
    mixed
6 whole cloves
a good pinch of ground
    cinnamon

Put the prunes and apricots in a bowl, and pour over the water – they should be covered. Leave to soak overnight.

Next morning, drain well, reserving the liquid. Put the soaked fruit in an ovenproof dish with the raisins or sultanas and the grapes. Add the bananas, pour the orange and apricot juice and the reserved liquid over the fruit, then add the cloves and cinnamon, and stir gently. Cook in a preheated oven, gas mark 6 (200°C/400°F), for 30-35 minutes until the fruit begins to soften. Serve warm or cold with a pot of yoghurt.

POACHED PLUMS WITH HONEY

Serves 4

450 g (1 lb) ripe dessert
    plums, halved and stoned

grated rind and juice of 2
    oranges
1-2 tablespoons clear honey

Place the plums in an ovenproof dish. Sprinkle with the grated rind and juice of the oranges. Dribble the honey over to taste. Bake in a preheated oven, gas mark 5 (190°C/375°F), for 20-25 minutes until tender. Serve hot or cold.

Muesli

Muesli has superseded other breakfast cereals in many households. It can be bought readily in most supermarkets and wholefood shops, but do check the labels before making your purchase as many brands contain a large amount of refined sugar. It isn't difficult to make muesli at home although I don't know whether it works out any cheaper than buying it ready-made and prepacked. Ideally, you need to use five different flakes (porridge oats, jumbo oats, barley flakes, rye flakes and wheat flakes) to ensure a good range of textures, flavours and nutrients. Having mixed the flakes together to form the base, add an assortment of chopped dried fruits and nuts to taste. It is usual to serve muesli with milk but I also like to soak it overnight in a little water or fruit juice. All the liquid should have been absorbed by the morning and, topped with fresh fruit and yoghurt, it makes a less chewy but equally delicious start to the day.

GOLDEN CRUNCHY MUESLI

Makes 675 g (1½ lb)

450 g (1 lb) jumbo oats
2 tablespoons sunflower oil
50 g (2 oz) sunflower seeds
50 g (2 oz) desiccated
 coconut
50 g (2 oz) chopped
 hazelnuts

a few drops of vanilla essence
1-2 tablespoons
 concentrated apple juice
100 g (4 oz) raisins *or*
 sultanas

Put the oats, oil, sunflower seeds, desiccated coconut and hazelnuts into a bowl. Add a few drops of vanilla essence, and sweeten to taste with concentrated apple juice. Mix together well. Spread the mixture thinly on a baking tray, and bake in a preheated oven, gas mark 5 (190°C/375°F), for 20–25 minutes, turning frequently to ensure even browning. When golden-brown, remove from the oven and leave to cool. Stir in the raisins or sultanas, and store in an airtight jar.

PORRIDGE

No self-respecting Scot would dream of making porridge with anything other than oatmeal, but, for the purist, even that isn't sufficient to guarantee a good product. F. Marian McNeill, the doyenne of traditional Scottish cookery, recommended using fresh spring water and coarsely ground meal, preferably home-milled, as she was convinced that modern mass-produced methods destroyed the essential goodness of the meal. Her method for making porridge was as follows: 'Allow for each person a breakfastcupful of water, a handful of oatmeal (about an ounce and a quarter) and a small saltspoonful of salt. Bring the water to the boil, and just as it approaches boiling point, add the oatmeal, letting it fall in a steady rain from the left hand whilst you stir it briskly with a spurtle (porridge-stick) or wooden spoon. When the porridge is boiling steadily, draw the pot to the side and put on the lid. Let it cook for from 20–30 minutes, according to the quality of the oatmeal. Let it cook for at least 10 minutes before you add the salt, which has a tendency to harden the meal and prevent it swelling if added at once. On the other hand, never cook porridge without salt. Ladle straight into cold porringers or soup-plates, and serve with small individual bowls of rich milk or thin cream. Each spoonful of porridge should be dipped and cooled in the milk or cream before being conveyed to the mouth.' (F. Marian McNeill, *The Book of Breakfasts*, Reprographia Edinburgh 1975.)

BREAKFAST ROLLS

Makes 8

350 g (12 oz) strong brown
  bread flour
15 g (½ oz) fresh yeast *or*
  7 g (¼ oz) dried yeast
200 ml (7 fl oz) warm milk
  (½ **boiling**/½ **cold**)

salt to taste
1 tablespoon sunflower oil
1 egg, beaten
oil as required
milk to glaze

Put a handful of the flour into a small bowl. Blend the fresh yeast into the warm milk or reconstitute the dried yeast as directed on the packet. Add the yeast liquid to the flour, and mix together. Leave in a warm place until frothy.

Put the remaining flour in a large bowl, and add salt to taste. Rub in the oil. Pour in the frothy yeast mixture and the beaten egg. Mix to form a soft dough, then turn on to a lightly floured surface, and knead until smooth and elastic. Divide the dough into eight pieces, and shape into rolls, tucking the edges underneath to prevent them from losing their shape. Place on an oiled baking tray, and leave in a warm place to rise. When doubled in size, brush with milk. Bake in a preheated oven, gas mark 6 (200°C/400°F), for 20 minutes until lightly browned and hollow-sounding when tapped on the bottom. Brush with a little more milk, and stand on a wire rack. Cover with a cloth, and leave to cool.

QUICK MUFFINS

A popular Victorian breakfast dish.

Makes 12

225 g (8 oz) strong brown
   bread flour
1 tablespoon sugar
1 level tablespoon baking
   powder

1 egg
250 ml (9 fl oz) milk
3 tablespoons sunflower oil

Put the flour, sugar and baking powder in a bowl, and mix together well. Put the egg, milk and oil into a small bowl, and beat together with a fork. Pour the liquid ingredients into the flour, and mix well (do not beat the mixture nor worry if the mixture looks slightly lumpy). Spoon into greased muffin or bun tins, and bake in a preheated oven, gas mark 6 (200°C/400°F), for 20–25 minutes until well risen. Test the centre of the muffins with a thin skewer; if it comes out clean they are ready. Cool for 5–10 minutes before cutting in half and spreading with butter. Serve with a pot of jam, and eat while warm.

Sunday Morning

Marmalade

There is no mistaking the Seville orange – it has a rough, tough, mottled skin which is in marked contrast to the near perfect skins of the sweet varieties. The flesh of each fruit is equally off-putting, being full of pith and seeds and tasting excruciatingly bitter. The passion for marmalade seems to be peculiarly British, and Seville oranges are exceedingly difficult to buy in their native Spain.

Marmalade comes from the Portuguese word *marmelo* meaning quince. Thick fruit preserves have been popular throughout the Mediterranean for hundreds of years, and similar recipes can be found in some of our old cookery books, but marmalades as we know them today, made exclusively from citrus fruits (oranges, lemons, limes and grapefruit), are a nineteenth-century creation and are attributed to a Mrs Keiller of Dundee. Her husband, a grocer, is reported to have purchased a cargo of Seville oranges, possibly mistaking them for sweet oranges and consequently had great difficulty selling them. In fact, they became something of an embarrassment and financial liability, and Mrs Keiller was obliged to use them herself. Following her mother's recipe for quince marmelat, she made an orange preserve which was an immediate success, and quickly established itself as the breakfast preserve *par excellence*. I use my aunt's recipe, and although the process is fairly lengthy, it is well worth the effort as the marmalade is wonderfully dark and thick. I have experimented with various sugar-free and low-sugar recipes but the results are never as good.

OXFORD MARMALADE

Makes 8–10 jars

1.5 kg (3 lb) Seville oranges	2.7 litres (5 pints) water
2 lemons	3 kg (6 lb) sugar

Put the fruit in a large pan with the water, cover and bring to the boil. Simmer for 2 hours, then leave to cool.

When the fruit is cool enough to handle, cut in half, scoop out the fleshy inside and put into a basin lined with butter muslin. Tie up the muslin so that the pips cannot escape and put into the pan. Pour any juice left in the basin into the pan too. Finely chop the orange and lemon skins, and return to the pan. Stand the pan over a moderate heat, and stir in the sugar. Heat until it has dissolved, and then remove from the heat. Leave to stand overnight.

Next day, bring the pan to the boil, and cook for 5 minutes. Remove the muslin bag, and hang it over the pan. Leave to drip overnight, and then discard. Boil rapidly until setting point is reached. Pour into clean jars, cover and label.

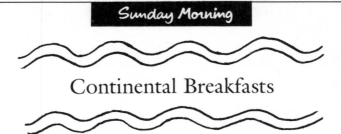

Continental Breakfasts

Visitors from the Continent are said to turn their back on rolls and coffee as soon as they cross the Channel, preferring instead to eat our full English breakfast of eggs, bacon, sausage and tomatoes. Novelty and the thrill of eating 'foreign' food must influence their choice, but so too must the all-too-familiar offering of microwaved rolls, insipid instant coffee, clingfilm-wrapped pats of butter and portions of jam – certainly not my idea of a Continental breakfast. It would seem that others agree with me if we are to believe Alan Bennett. Recently, while appearing on a popular radio programme, he recounted a conversation he overheard in the dining-room of a seaside hotel on the south coast. It took place between the waiter and a rather large lady from Yorkshire. When asked whether she would prefer an English or Continental breakfast, the lady replied, 'Oh, I don't want any of that foreign rubbish. Bring me rolls, jam and coffee please.'

CROISSANTS

Most supermarkets and high-class bakers sell croissants these days but they are pale imitations of the real thing, being made with a fat other than butter. If you cannot buy good croissants, it is worth making your own as they keep well in the freezer. I have made them successfully with both brown and white flours.

The best, and, to my mind, only way to eat croissants, is warm from the oven with a large cup of milky coffee. The current vogue for cutting them in half, toasting them and then spreading each slice with yet more butter and a generous dollop of jam seems a trifle excessive.

Makes 12

450 g (1 lb) strong bread flour
25 g (1 oz) fresh yeast *or* 15 g (½ oz) dried yeast
225 ml (8 fl oz) warm water (½ boiling/½ cold)

a pinch of salt (optional)
1 egg, beaten
175 g (6 oz) soft butter
beaten egg or milk to glaze

Put a handful of the measured flour into a small bowl, blend the fresh yeast into the warm water or reconstitute the dried yeast as directed on the packet. Add the yeast liquid to the flour, and mix together. Leave in a warm place until frothy. Put the remaining flour in a larger bowl, add the salt, if using it, the frothy yeast and beaten egg. Mix to form a dough, and knead until smooth and elastic. Roll out to form a rectangle measuring 50 × 20 cm (20 × 8 inches). Divide the butter into three portions. Dot one portion over two-thirds of the rolled-out dough. Mark the dough into three sections, taking care not to cut through it completely. Fold the unbuttered section over the middle section and then the last buttered section over that. Press the edges together to seal, and turn through 90°. Roll out gently to form another rectangle. Dot with another portion of butter, fold, turn and roll out again. Cover with the remaining portion of butter, and fold once more. Wrap in clingfilm, and chill in the refrigerator for 30 minutes. Roll out the dough to form another rectangle, and fold over the three sections as before, without adding any butter. Repeat this rolling and folding twice more before putting to chill for a further hour.

Roll out to form a rectangle measuring 55 × 30 cm (22 × 12 inches). Cut in half lengthways, and then cut each strip into three squares. Finally, cut each square in half diagonally to form two triangles. Roll up each triangle loosely, starting at the base and finishing with the tip of the triangle underneath the roll. Repeat using all 12 pieces of dough. Place the rolls on a lightly buttered baking tray, and twist each one to form a crescent. Cover and put in a warm place to double in size. Brush with beaten egg or milk. Bake in a preheated oven, gas mark 8 (230°C/ 450°F), for 20–25 minutes until golden-brown and hollow-sounding when tapped on the bottom. Cool on a wire rack.

BRIOCHE

A light, rich bread which has a almost cake-like texture. It is delicious eaten warm or even toasted for breakfast. Traditionally, brioche is baked in a deep, fluted mould but it tastes just as good shaped as a cottage loaf and baked on a flat tray.

Makes 1 loaf

275 g (10 oz) unbleached white flour
a pinch of salt (optional)
2 teaspoons sugar
15 g (½ oz) fresh yeast *or* 7 g (¼ oz) dried yeast

75 ml (3 fl oz) warm milk (½ boiling/½ cold)
75 g (3 oz) soft butter
milk to glaze

Sift the flour, salt, if using it, and the sugar into a mixing bowl. Blend the fresh yeast into the warm milk or reconstitute the dried yeast as directed on the packet. Leave in a warm place until frothy. Make a well in the flour, and pour in the yeast mixture and the eggs. Mix together to form a dough, then knead until smooth and elastic. Working on a lightly floured surface, roll out until 0.6 cm (¼ inch) thick. Divide the butter into three parts, and dab a third of it over the dough. Knead again until the butter is worked into the dough. Repeat the process twice more until all the butter has been incorporated. Return to the bowl, cover and leave in a warm place for 1–2 hours until well risen.

Knead the dough again for several minutes. Place in fluted brioche tins or divide into two pieces, one slightly larger than the other. Roll into two balls, and place the larger one on a greased baking tray. Put the smaller one on top of the larger piece of dough to form a cottage loaf. Make a hole through the centre of the loaf by pushing in the handle of a wooden spoon. Leave in a warm place until well risen, then brush with milk. Bake in a preheated oven, gas mark 6 (200°C/400°F), for 30 minutes until golden-brown and hollow-sounding when tapped on the bottom. Cool on a wire rack.

Sunday Morning

Smoked Fish

'In the breakfast, the Scots, whether of the Lowlands or mountains, must be confessed to excel us. The tea and coffee are accompanied not only with butter, but with honey, conserves and marmalades. If an epicure could remove by a wish in quest of sensual gratification, wherever he had supped, he would breakfast in Scotland.' Perhaps Dr Johnson was also thinking of Scottish kippers, Arbroath smokies and Finnan haddock, when he wrote these words for they alone are worthy of a journey north of the border.

The traditional Scottish method of cooking kippers is to lay them in a frying pan without any fat. Cover and cook over a gentle heat for 5-10 minutes, turning once. In this way, they will cook to perfection in their own oils. They can also be cooked under a hot grill or in a preheated oven. However, I prefer jugging kippers by placing them in a container of boiling water as it stops the whole house being filled with their smell which can, after the initial tantalizing whiff, outstay its welcome.

Although one American writer described the kipper as 'the king of the English breakfast', my personal favourite is smoked haddock, sold either as Finnan haddock or Arbroath smokies. Both are lighter in flavour and texture than the kipper and are easier on the digestive system. Arbroath smokies should be heated through under a hot grill or in a preheated oven and served with a knob of butter. Finnan haddock can also be grilled but its traditional breakfast role is in Kedgeree.

KEDGEREE

Kedgeree can be made the day before, then heated in the oven as and when needed.

Serves 4

450 g (1 lb) Finnan haddock	275 g (10 oz) cooked long
a knob of butter	grain brown rice
1 onion, finely chopped	freshly ground black pepper
1 teaspoon curry powder	1–2 tablespoons chopped
2 hard–boiled eggs, chopped	fresh parsley

Grill the fish for 5–7 minutes until tender. When cool enough to handle, remove the skin and bones, and break the fish into large flakes. Keep warm.

Meanwhile, melt the butter in a frying pan, and sauté the onion for 5–7 minutes until soft and golden. Add the curry powder, and cook for a minute or two more, stirring all the time.

Put the onion, flaked fish, chopped eggs and cooked rice in a bowl, and mix together carefully. Season to taste with black pepper and parsley. Spoon into a shallow, ovenproof dish, and heat through in a moderate to hot oven, turning occasionally.

JUGGED KIPPERS

Stand the fish, tail uppermost, in a tall jug, and cover with boiling water so that just the inedible tail protrudes. Leave to stand for 5-10 minutes until heated through. Take hold of the fish's tail, and lift out of the jug. Drain and pat dry with absorbent paper. Serve hot.

Potato Dishes

Some of the best breakfast foods are made from yesterday's leftovers. Cooked potatoes, in particular, can be used to great advantage.

SAUTÉED POTATOES

Slice any leftover boiled potatoes, and sauté in hot shallow fat, turning occasionally, until golden-brown and crisp on the outside. Drain on absorbent paper before serving.

POTATO PATTIES

Shape any leftover mashed potato into thin cakes. Fry in shallow fat until speckled brown on both sides.

COD'S ROE AND POTATO SCONES

Mix together equal amounts of peeled cod's roe and mashed potato. Season to taste, and bind with beaten egg. Shape into thin cakes, and fry in shallow fat, turning once, until golden-brown.

POTATO SCONES

Thicken up any leftover mashed potato with a little flour. Use approximately 100 g (4 oz) for every 450 g (1 lb) mashed potato. Season to taste. Roll out to approximately 1.25 cm (½ inch) thick, and cut into triangles or rounds. Fry in shallow fat until browned on both sides.

Eggs

No Victorian breakfast table was complete without a dish of eggs, and a common saying among the cooks of the period was, 'if he don't eat fish he can always take an egg'. Boiling or coddling were the two principal ways of cooking breakfast eggs, and various devices were used to ensure that the eggs stayed hot throughout the meal. Some households had egg-boilers which cooked each egg at the table, others used decorative china hens filled with hot water while 'breakfast trays' and single gents had egg cosies.

CODDLED EGGS

Put the eggs in a pan of boiling water, cover and reduce the heat until the water is barely stirring. Cook for 6–7 minutes by which time the white will have set and the yolk will be deliciously creamy. Coddled eggs are said to be more digestible than boiled ones. They can be kept for some time in hot water without becoming hard and rubbery.

OEUFS SUR LE PLAT

Lightly butter four small, ovenproof dishes. Carefully break an egg into each one, and sprinkle with salt and pepper to taste. Dot with butter, and bake in a preheated oven, gas mark 6 (200°C/400°F), for 7–9 minutes until the white has set.

Alternatively, chop a little bacon and a few mushrooms into the base of each dish, and cook in the preheated oven for 5-7 minutes before adding the eggs and continue to cook as directed above.

BACON AND EGGS

For most people, a plate of bacon and eggs epitomizes the traditional British breakfast. So popular has the combination proved to be that cookery writer Margaret Costa declares that it is her favourite desert island dish, while her Scottish counterpart F. Marian McNeill wrote, 'the marriage of bacon and eggs was certainly made in heaven.'

Everyone, I am sure, has their own particular way of preparing this dish; some people like their bacon crisp and their eggs turned and fringed with gold, while others prefer the bacon to be pink and their eggs soft and sunnyside up. While I don't think it necessary to give cooking instructions, I will offer one piece of advice which I have found very useful and that is to nick the bacon fat in several places as this prevents the rashers curling up during cooking.

Bacon and eggs can be served on their own or with kidneys, sausages, cod's roe, black pudding, haggis, tomatoes, mushrooms, fried bread and potato cakes; in fact with almost anything that takes your fancy. Black pudding and haggis may seem unusual breakfast foods but I can heartily recommend them. Cut both into thick slices, and cook with the bacon under a hot grill or in the frying pan.

Beverages

Tea, coffee and chocolate were not introduced into Britain until the middle of the seventeenth century. Coffee was the first of these drinks to reach our shores and it was an immediate success. Britain quickly became the greatest coffee drinking nation of Europe. However, its introduction did not please everyone, the principal objectors being innkeepers and women. Clearly, innkeepers were fearful of losing their livelihood while women lived in fear of losing their husbands as they themselves were barred from the fashionable coffee houses which were springing up in all the major towns and cities. The wives of coffee drinkers were also convinced that the beverage itself made their menfolk as 'unfruitful as the desert where that unhappy berry is said to be bought'.

Well it wasn't long, however, before coffee was being challenged by the introduction of tea. Royalty and the well-to-do were drinking pots of tea for breakfast as early as 1702 but it wasn't until the mid-eighteenth century that the price fell sufficiently to enable working-class folk to enjoy this new beverage. As a result, the coffee houses were forced to throw open their doors to women and began selling tea as well. Philanthropic firms, such as the Quaker companies of Fry's and Cadbury's, began serving tea and biscuits free of charge to girls who turned up early for work. Considering the nature of their business activities, I am surprised that they did not provide hot chocolate!

Although chocolate drinks are acceptable alternatives to tea and coffee elsewhere in Europe, they have never really been taken seriously in this country. By far the best method of making a chocolate drink is with real chocolate. 'The milk was boiling on the blue-tiled charcoal stove. Nearby, a bar of chocolate was melting in a little water for my breakfast', (Colette, *Earthly Paradise*, Penguin Books 1974). The hot milk would be stirred into the melted chocolate, brought to the boil and poured, piping hot and frothy, into a waiting cup.

COFFEE

With so many books available, covering every conceivable aspect of buying, roasting, grinding and making coffee, I don't feel remiss in omitting to discuss technical details here. Claudia Roden sums up the pertinent points in her excellent book *Coffee* (Penguin Books 1981) by saying, 'preserving the fragrance and the fleeting aroma is what good coffee is about, and the secret, as the pundits often repeat, lies in the word, "fresh"; freshly roasted, freshly ground and freshly made.'

Few of us have the time, patience or equipment to roast our own beans but there is no reason why we should not grind them at home, and it is well worth investing in a coffee grinder. Although coffee beans retain their aroma longer than ground coffee, the same golden rule applies to both – buy little and often. Some people suggest that the shelf-life of coffee can be increased by storing it, in sealed containers, in a refrigerator or freezer but I have not found either particularly satisfactory.

There is nothing mysterious or difficult about making a good cup of coffee. The first thing to remember is that boiling the grounds makes the coffee very bitter and, though the Turks and Italians seem to like it this way, most people prefer to let their coffee infuse in either a percolator, filter or jug. By far the simplest method is to use a jug or pot, and to make the coffee in exactly the same way as you would make a pot of tea, using 1 tablespoon of ground coffee per person. It is important to grind the beans to the correct degree; if using a filter, they need to be finely ground, but should be left a little coarser if making the coffee in a jug or percolator.

CAFÉ AU LAIT

This is the French breakfast drink; it is best served in wide brimmed cups – large enough to wrap your hands around.

Using medium-roasted beans, make some extra strong coffee, and bring some creamy milk to the boil in a saucepan. Pour the strained coffee into a cup, and top up with hot milk. The proportion of coffee to milk depends very much on personal taste. Sprinkle a little grated chocolate, nutmeg, orange peel or ground cinnamon over the top if desired.

Sunday Lunch

Roast Lunch

Mange-tout

Carrots

Sunday Lunch

The English passion for roast meat is acknowledged throughout the world and it is one area of cooking in which we excel. No other country can rival our Sunday lunches with their joints of meat, sauces and gravies. While the tradition of serving apple sauce with pork is not uniquely British, the same cannot be said of roast beef and Yorkshire pudding and lamb with mint sauce. Oddly enough, mint sauce is the accompaniment that has caused most consternation among our friends and rivals overseas. The great American cookery writer, M. F. K. Fisher, describes it as a 'horrid douse' while Dumas, the nineteenth-century French philosopher, and gourmet, said 'to go so far as to discuss rare beef [sic] with mint sauce which is the delight of certain foreign tables would be beneath us, for we are concerned with honesty and reason, not with barbarity.'

With so many references being made to 'the beef of old England', it is hardly surprising that today we have the impression that meat was eaten at every meal and that the spit with its huge joint of meat was the focal point of medieval and tudor kitchens. In fact, nothing could be further from the truth; only the wealthiest families were able to afford beef, lamb, mutton and pork with any degree of regularity and it was not until the late eighteenth century that the situation changed. At this time, it became both practical and viable to over-winter cattle rather than slaughtering all but the breeding stock at the onset of the cold weather. On the domestic front, the first solid fuel ranges went into production complete with brick ovens and hot plates, a development viewed with horror by traditionalists who predicted that it would mean the end of the British roast, claiming that the new ovens would necessitate the use of smaller joints of meat with a resulting loss of flavour and, worse still, the meat would be baked rather than roasted. Elisabeth Ayrton in her excellent book, *Cookery of England* (Penguin Books, 1974) noted that 'with the development of the cooking stove and the range, spits went out of use and the taste of the fire went with them. Joints of meat were worse cooked than ever before in a country noted for the pleasure it took in the excellence and abundance of its meat.' Thankfully, she follows on by saying that joints can be cooked excellently in modern ovens.

One of the chief concerns today, however, is not whether the roast is authentically cooked but whether one can afford to buy the meat in the first place. When I was a girl, a Sunday joint was the norm. Even allowing for shrinkage, it was larger than necessary as it was customary to serve the leftovers cold with pickles and fried potatoes on the following day. It may even have stretched to make a sandwich or two,

Sunday Lunch

but never 'hashed on Tuesday, minced on Wednesday, curried on Thursday, broth on Friday and cottage pie on Saturday.'

Apart from cost, there is another less obvious reason why fewer families are sitting down to a traditional Sunday lunch – namely that of health. In recent years, the number of vegetarians has been growing steadily and many more people are becoming selective about the type and amount of meat they eat. With meat products accounting for a quarter of the saturated fat content in a typical diet, and Britain's rate of heart disease ranked the highest in the world, there have been numerous calls for us to reduce our consumption of fat, in particular, saturated animal fats. However, it doesn't follow that we should give up eating meat altogether. Joints are preferable to processed meats such as sausages, pies and many minced meat products which have higher levels of saturated fat.

Another principal concern relates to the widespread use of antibiotics and hormones in animals. Those worried about this issue can, of course, abstain from eating meat or buy it from an organic supplier but many people find themselves having to make a compromise and, while continuing to eat meat, they prefer to eat lamb or game which are thought to have lower residues than intensively reared pork, beef or chicken.

Combine the recipes in this chapter with the starters and puddings on pages 57 to 69 and 92 to 100 and Sunday lunch takes on a truly festive air.

Chicken

The great eighteenth-century gourmet and philosopher Brillat-Savarin said, 'a chicken is a canvas on which the cook can paint' and it is easy to see what he meant. Chicken is one of the most versatile of foods and is an excellent vehicle for many different flavours. At one time or another, it has been seasoned, basted, marinated, stuffed or garnished with almost every conceivable food including bacon, tomatoes, spicy garlic sausages (*chorizos*), crab, fennel, walnuts, pine kernels, limes, oysters, pineapple, saffron, cream and yoghurt. Don't assume, however, that chicken always needs embellishment. A good chicken, plainly roasted, needs little in the way of accompaniments and is delicious served simply with a green salad and new potatoes, particularly if a sprig or two of tarragon, thyme or marjoram are put inside the bird before it is cooked.

Gone are the days when fowl were specially fattened for the roasting tin, and although intensive rearing has produced a cheaper, more uniform product, the quality is not always as good. The birds are now fattened so quickly that their flavour has little time to develop with the result that many are dull and insipid. Free-range farm chickens are generally considered to have the finest flavour, but be warned, they may not look as attractive or as succulent as the plump-breasted birds we are accustomed to seeing, and you do need to buy a bigger bird than usual. A good compromise is to buy fresh chickens, the sort that are sold plucked and trussed in family butchers. Their flavour and texture is usually very good, and I find them ideal for roasting, grilling and frying. They should, however, be cooked on the day of purchase.

By far the most common type of chicken available in our shops is that sold from the freezer cabinets, tightly sealed inside a polythene bag. Such birds are cheap, plentiful and very useful but the flesh can be rather characterless and I prefer to use them in stews, casseroles, soups and pies or stuffed with a savoury filling. Frozen chicken is well worth buying but do remember to thaw it out thoroughly before cooking, either in a refrigerator or in a cool room. Some large supermarkets are also selling maize-fed chickens which can easily be recognized by their corn-coloured flesh. Their flavour is fine and delicate and, while they are certainly superior to the average chicken, they are not necessarily as good as a true free-range bird.

Sunday Lunch

Ironically, familiarity has bred contempt, and nowadays people consider a piece of lamb, pork, beef or game to be a more worthy and acceptable dish for Sunday lunch or a special occasion. However, consumption of chicken is still rising, due in part to its reasonable price but also to the increasing number of people who are switching to white meat for health reasons, as it has a much lower fat content than most red meats. Economics and health aside, I don't think we should underestimate the usefulness and versatility of chicken.

COUNTRY CHICKEN

Serves 4–6

½ lemon
2–3 sprigs of fresh thyme
1 oven-ready chicken
   weighing 1.2–1.3 kg
   (2½–2¾ lb)

2 tablespoons olive oil
2 teaspoons Dijon mustard

Put the lemon and thyme inside the chicken. Place in a roasting tin. Mix together the olive oil and mustard and brush this over the outside of the bird. Roast in a preheated oven, gas mark 6 (200°C/400°F), for 1¼–1½ hours until the chicken is tender. Test the chicken by pricking the breast with a thin skewer – when the juices run clear rather than red, the chicken is ready.

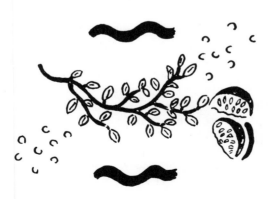

CHICKEN STUFFED WITH APRICOTS AND ALMONDS

An impressive way to serve chicken.

Serves 4-6

1 oven-ready chicken
weighing 1.2-1.3 kg
(2½-2¾ lb)

FOR THE STUFFING
100 g (4 oz) dried apricots,
chopped
275 ml (½ pint) water
4 tablespoons sunflower oil
1 onion, chopped
25 g (1 oz) blanched
almonds, sliced

3-4 tablespoons fresh
wholewheat breadcrumbs
1 tablespoon chopped fresh
parsley
a good pinch of ground
cinnamon
a good pinch of ground
cloves
grated rind of a small lemon
salt, pepper

Lay the chicken, breast down, and, using a strong knife, cut down each side of the breastbone from the neck to the parson's nose. Working downwards, carefully cut the skin and flesh away from the carcass. When you reach the thigh sockets, push the knife into the joint, and twist to break the joint. Free the wing bones in the same manner. Continue to cut down and around the carcass until you are able to lift it free. Starting from inside the chicken, ease the knife down each leg, working the bone free. Do the same to free the wing bones. The bird should now be free of bones but still in one piece and ready for stuffing.

To make the stuffing, put the apricots in a small pan with the water. Cover and simmer gently for 30 minutes until they soften, adding more water if necessary. Heat 1 tablespoon of oil in another pan, and sauté the onion, for 5-7 minutes until it begins to soften. Stir in the almonds, and continue to cook until they begin to brown. Remove the pan from the heat, then add the breadcrumbs, parsley, cinnamon, cloves and grated lemon rind. Drain the apricots and reserve the juice. Put the apricots into the stuffing mixture along with 3 tablespoons of their cooking juices. Mix together well, and season to taste.

Fill the bird with the stuffing, taking care not to pack it too tightly or the skin may burst as it is cooking. Sew up the opening with string, and push the bird into shape. Heat the remaining oil in a casserole-type pan, and brown the chicken on all sides. Cover and transfer to a preheated oven, gas mark 4 (180°C/350°F), for 1 hour, basting occasionally.

CHICKEN CASSEROLE SPICED WITH CUMIN

Cumin looks rather like caraway and the two are often confused. Their flavours, however, are as different as chalk and cheese. Cumin is a spice, which is very popular around the Mediterranean. It is not a hot spice but is used for its sweet, slightly nutty taste.

Serves 4

1 clove of garlic, peeled and
   crushed
2 tablespoons olive oil
juice of 3 lemons
½ teaspoon cumin seeds
1 oven-ready chicken,
   weighing 1.2 kg (2½ lb)

25 g (1 oz) butter
1 onion, chopped
2–3 sprigs of fresh thyme
freshly ground black pepper
grated zest of 1 lemon

Put the garlic, olive oil, lemon juice and cumin seeds in a large bowl and mix together well. Joint the chicken and remove the skin. Put the pieces into the bowl and leave to marinate in a cool place for several hours, turning occasionally.

Melt the butter in a casserole-type pan, and sauté the onion gently for 5–7 minutes until soft and golden. Remove the chicken pieces from the marinade with a slotted spoon and put into the pan. Brown evenly on all sides. Pour the marinade over and add the thyme. Season to taste with black pepper. Bring to the boil, cover and simmer gently for 45–55 minutes until tender. Adjust the seasoning to taste and sprinkle with lemon zest before serving.

Serve with brown rice. I like to follow the chicken and rice with a salad made from watercress, tomatoes, grated carrot and grated celeriac. I ensure that 2–3 tablespoons of the lemon and cumin sauce remain at the end of the main course and pour this over the salad at the table. Toss lightly before serving.

CHICKEN WITH MUSHROOMS AND RED WINE

Serves 4-6

2-3 tablespoons olive oil
1 onion, finely chopped
100 g (4 oz) button
  mushrooms, chopped
1 clove of garlic, peeled and
  crushed
1 oven-ready chicken
  weighing 1.2-1.3 kg
  (2½-2¾ lb)

150 ml (¼ pint) red wine
juice of 1 lemon
2 tablespoons chopped fresh
  thyme
salt, pepper

Heat the oil in a large casserole-type pan, and sauté the onion for 5-7 minutes until soft and golden. Add the mushrooms and garlic, and continue to cook for a further 2-3 minutes, stirring frequently. Remove the vegetables with a slotted spoon and keep aside until needed.

Put the chicken into the pan, and brown on all sides, adding more oil if necessary. Return the onion and mushrooms to the pan. Pour the wine and lemon juice over, then add the thyme. Cover with a tight-fitting lid, and simmer for 45-55 minutes until the bird is tender. Check the pan towards the end of cooking to make sure that it is not boiling dry; add a little water if necessary. Season to taste before serving.

PIGEONS WITH FRESH GARDEN PEAS

Pigeons have a pleasant beefy flavour. When young, they are succulent and tender and can be roasted in 10–15 minutes. Older birds, however, take a good deal longer to cook and, as it is difficult, if not impossible, to tell the age of a trussed, oven-ready bird, I suggest you play safe and cook the birds slowly in stews and casseroles.

This is a classic French dish best made in the summer when there is a plentiful supply of fresh garden peas. There is a good deal of wastage with fresh peas and you'll need to buy 1.8 kg (4 lb) of peas in the pod for this recipe. Don't throw away the empty pods. If cooked with some onion, celery, carrot, potato, herbs, milk and water, and perhaps a rasher or two of bacon, they make the basis for an acceptable soup. Rub through a sieve before adjusting the consistency and seasoning to taste and pouring into a soup tureen.

Serves 4

2–3 tablespoons olive oil	75 ml (3 fl oz) water
175 g (6 oz) lean unsmoked bacon, trimmed and chopped	450 g (1 lb) shelled peas
2 onions, chopped	1 crisp lettuce heart, shredded
4 oven-ready pigeons	2 sprigs of fresh parsley
200 ml (7 fl oz) dry white wine	2 sprigs of fresh thyme
	1 bay leaf
	salt, pepper

Heat 1–2 tablespoons of the oil in a large casserole-type pan, and sauté the bacon and onions for 5–7 minutes. Remove from the pan with a slotted spoon and keep aside until needed.

Brown the pigeons in the remaining oil, then pour the wine over. Return the sautéed bacon and onions to the pan along with the water, peas, lettuce, parsley, thyme and bay leaf. Bring to the boil, cover with a tight-fitting lid, and simmer gently for 1¼–1½ hours until the pigeons are tender. Check the pan occasionally during the cooking to make sure that it is not boiling dry; add a little more water if necessary.

Lift the pigeons from the pan, and arrange on a serving dish. Discard the herbs, then stir the cooked vegetable mixture well to loosen any meat juices which may be sticking to the bottom of the pan. Season to taste, and spoon this around the birds.

Sunday Lunch

COUNTRY-STYLE PARTRIDGE

Serves 4

2-3 tablespoons sunflower
  oil
2 oven-ready partridges,
  halved
100 g (4 oz) lean unsmoked
  bacon, trimmed and
  chopped
2 onions, chopped
350 g (12 oz) white cabbage,
  shredded

2 sticks of celery, chopped
2 carrots, sliced
275 ml (½ pint) dry white
  wine
1 bay leaf
2-3 sprigs of fresh thyme
freshly ground black pepper

Heat the oil in a casserole-type pan, and brown the partridges, on all sides. Remove from the pan with a slotted spoon and keep aside until needed.

Add the bacon and the onions to the pan and sauté for 4-5 minutes. Add the remaining vegetables, and cook for a minute or two more, stirring frequently. Return the partridges to the pan and pour the wine over. Add the herbs, then cover with a tight-fitting lid, and cook in a preheated oven, gas mark 5 (190°C/375°F), for 1½-1¾ hours until the birds are tender. Remove the herbs, and season with black pepper. Stir a little water into the pan if all the stock has been absorbed during cooking.

PHEASANT WITH CHESTNUTS

A delicious combination of flavours and textures, and the perfect dish for a cold winter's day.

Serves 3–4

450 g (1 lb) chestnuts	150 ml (¼ pint) red wine
2–3 tablespoons sunflower oil	275 ml (½ pint) game *or* chicken stock (see page 156)
4 shallots *or* 1 small onion, chopped	½ stick of celery, chopped
100 g (4 oz) cup mushrooms, chopped	1 sprig of fresh parsley
1 young plump oven–ready pheasant	1 sprig of fresh thyme
	1 bay leaf
	salt, pepper

Using a sharp knife, make a slit in the concave side of each chestnut. Place in a small pan, cover with water and bring to the boil. Cook for 10 minutes. Drain well and cover with cold water. Peel immediately, removing both the hard outer and the inner brown shells. Set aside until needed.

Heat the oil in a heavy, casserole-type pan, and sauté the shallots or onion, for several minutes until they begin to brown and soften. Add the mushrooms, and cook for several minutes more. Remove the vegetables from the pan with a slotted spoon, and set aside until needed.

Put the bird into the pan, and brown on all sides. Return the sautéed vegetables to the pan, and pour the wine and stock over. Add the celery and herbs. Bring to the boil, reduce to a simmer, cover with a tight-fitting lid, and cook for 25 minutes. Turn the pheasant, then add the peeled chestnuts. Replace the lid, and cook for a further 15 minutes until the bird is tender. Remove the herbs, and season to taste before serving.

ROAST BEEF AND YORKSHIRE PUDDING

By far the best way to serve roast beef and Yorkshire pudding is in the traditional manner; that is, to eat the pudding first, as a separate course, followed by the meat and vegetables. This practice not only ensures that the light, golden, crusty pudding is enjoyed to the full but it is also a sly way of making the meat go a little further. Roast beef has never been cheap and yet, until recently, even the poorest families would pride themselves on being able to afford a Sunday joint. However, to buy a piece of meat at the weekend was one thing; letting the family eat it all up at one meal was quite another. To ensure that this did not happen, it is said that thrifty Yorkshire women hit upon the idea of serving this savoury pudding first in order to take the edge off their families' appetites before putting the costly joint on the table. This may well be true but I have never heard a Yorkshireman complain about the arrangement. In fact, a portion of Yorkshire pudding, served with lashings of good meaty gravy and perhaps some raspberry vinegar, is considered by most to be as good as the roast itself.

Serves 4–6

1.2–1.5 kg (2½–3 lb) rib of beef
vegetable oil as required

FOR THE YORKSHIRE PUDDING BATTER
100 g (4 oz) plain flour
salt, pepper
1 egg, beaten
275 ml (½ pint) milk

Put the meat on a lightly oiled roasting tin, fat side up. Roast in a preheated oven, gas mark 7 (220°C/425°F), for 70–80 minutes, basting occasionally.

Meanwhile, make the Yorkshire pudding batter. Put the flour in a bowl, and season to taste. Make a well in the centre, then add the egg and half the milk. Mix to form a smooth paste. Gradually add the rest of the milk, beating well after each addition. If necessary, thin down with water until the batter has the consistency of thick cream. If using a liquidizer or food processor, put all the ingredients into the goblet, and blend until smooth.

About 20 minutes before the meat is due to come out of the oven, collect a little of the fat from the bottom of the roasting tin, and spoon into 12 bun tins or into Yorkshire pudding tins. It may be necessary to use some vegetable oil too. Remember to leave sufficient meat juices in the roasting tin to make the gravy. Put the Yorkshire pudding tins in the oven, on a high shelf, and leave until the fat begins to smoke. Pour some batter into each, and then return to the oven. Keep back 1–2 tablespoons of batter as this is very useful for thickening the gravy. Bake the Yorkshire puddings for 15–25 minutes, depending on their size, until well risen and lightly browned around the edges. Make the gravy while the puddings are in the oven – 'a Yorkshire pudding waits for no man, like a soufflé, man must wait for the pudding'. Leave the meat in a warm place while the first course is being served. It will come to no harm; in fact it will be easier to carve after its rest.

POT ROAST BEEF WITH VEGETABLES

An excellent way to cook cheaper cuts of meat. It not only keeps them moist and succulent but also reduces shrinkage.

Serves 4

2–3 tablespoons sunflower oil	1 clove of garlic, peeled and crushed
675–750 g (1½–1¾ lb) rolled brisket of beef	275 ml (½ pint) water
2 onions, sliced	1 good teaspoon ready-made English mustard
2 carrots, sliced	salt, pepper
2 parsnips, sliced	

Heat the oil in a heavy casserole-type pan, and brown the meat on all sides. Remove from the pan, and keep aside until needed. Put the onions into the pan, and sauté for several minutes. Add the carrots, parsnips and garlic, and cook for 4–5 minutes, stirring frequently. Make a hollow in the centre of the vegetables, and lay the meat on top. Pour the water over, cover and cook in a preheated oven, gas mark 4 (180°C/350°F), for 2–2½ hours until the meat is tender, turning occasionally. Lift the meat on to a serving plate, and keep warm.

Stir the mustard into the vegetable mixture, and season to taste. Spoon some of the mixture around the joint, and serve the remainder in a tureen.

BOEUF À LA MODE

Serves 4-6

FOR THE MARINADE
275 ml (½ pint) red wine
3 carrots, sliced
1 small onion, chopped
1 sprig of fresh parsley
1 sprig of fresh thyme
1 bay leaf
**1 clove of garlic, peeled and
crushed**

FOR THE REMAINING INGREDIENTS
1.2 kg (2½ lb) topside of beef
2-3 tablespoons olive oil
**100 g (4 oz) lean, unsmoked
bacon, trimmed and
chopped**
**225 g (8 oz) button
mushrooms, halved if
necessary**
salt, pepper

To make the marinade, put the wine, carrots, onion, parsley, thyme, bay leaf and garlic in a bowl. Add the meat, and submerge as much as possible in the marinade. Cover and leave in a cool place for 24 hours, turning once.

Lift the meat from the marinade, and strain the liquid. Discard the solids. Heat the oil in a heavy, casserole-type pan, add the meat, and brown on all sides. Remove from the pan, and keep aside until needed. Put the bacon and mushrooms into the pan, and sauté for 3-4 minutes. Return the beef to the pan and pour the strained marinade over. Bring to the boil, cover and simmer for 2¼-2½ hours until tender. Season to taste before serving.

Sunday Lunch

ROAST LAMB WITH BUTTER BEAN PURÉE

Butter beans have been an accepted accompaniment to roast lamb since long before the current vogue for healthy eating. Whatever your reasons for choosing this recipe, I am sure you won't be disappointed.

Serves 4–6

175 g (6 oz) butter beans, soaked overnight and then drained	2 cloves of garlic, peeled and crushed
850 ml (1½ pints) water	salt, pepper
2 sticks of celery, chopped	olive oil
2 carrots, chopped	½ shoulder of lamb
4 sprigs of fresh rosemary	(weighing about 1.2 kg (2½ lb))

Using a large pan or pressure cooker, boil the beans briskly in the water for at least 10 minutes, then add the celery, carrots, rosemary and garlic. Cover and simmer for 1½–2 hours until tender, adding more water as and when necessary, or pressure-cook at *high* pressure for 20 minutes. Discard the sprigs of rosemary. Pass half the cooked beans through the coarse blade of a vegetable mouli or blend in a liquidizer or food processor with 275 ml (½ pint) bean stock. Return the puréed beans to the pan, and bring to the boil. Boil briskly, without covering, until the mixture is reduced to a coarse, thick purée. Season to taste, adding more chopped fresh rosemary if necessary.

Meanwhile, place the shoulder of lamb in an oiled roasting tin. Brush the meat lightly with oil, then roast in a preheated oven, gas mark 6 (200°C/400°F), for 1¼–1½ hours until the meat is tender, basting occasionally. Serve with the hot butter bean purée.

Sunday Lunch

SPICED LEG OF LAMB

Serves 4-6

1.2-1.3 kg (2½-2¾ lb) leg of
  lamb
2-3 tablespoons olive oil
2 level teaspoons ready-made
  English mustard
2 teaspoons white wine
  vinegar
1 teaspoon tomato purée
½ level teaspoon paprika

½ level teaspoon turmeric
½ level teaspoon chilli
  powder
½ level teaspoon ground
  mace
freshly ground black pepper
flour
water

Brush the lamb with olive oil, and place on a roasting tray. Cook in a preheated oven, gas mark 5 (190°C/375°F), for 30 minutes.

Meanwhile, put 1 tablespoon of oil in a small bowl, and add the mustard, wine vinegar, tomato purée and the spices.

Using a sharp knife, make a series of deep cuts in the lamb, and spread some of the mixture into each. Brush the remaining mixture over the joint, and return to the oven. Cook for a further 40-50 minutes until the meat is tender, basting occasionally. Lift from the pan, and put on to a serving dish. Keep warm.

To make the gravy, drain the fat from the roasting tin. Stir about 1 tablespoon of flour into the remaining pan juices. Thin down with water, stirring well after each addition. Heat through, and adjust the consistency and seasoning to taste.

MARINATED LEG OF LAMB

Serves 4–6

1.2–1.3 kg (2½–2¾ lb) leg of lamb

FOR THE STOCK
2–3 sprigs of fresh thyme
2–3 sprigs of fresh parsley
1 bay leaf
the green top of 1 leek, chopped
1 carrot, chopped
1 stick of celery, chopped
10 black peppercorns
water

FOR THE MARINADE
75 ml (3 fl oz) red wine
75 ml (3 fl oz) natural orange juice
50 ml (2 fl oz) olive oil
2–3 sprigs of fresh thyme
1 clove of garlic, peeled and crushed
a liberal sprinkling of black pepper

To bone the leg of lamb, place the joint, meaty side down, on a chopping board. Cut through the meat on top of the joint to expose the length of the bone. Cut the meat from around the bone until it is free and can be removed. Cut the thicker parts of the joint almost in half to make the joint a more even thickness. Trim off any excess fat.

Put the bones in a large pan with all the stock ingredients, barely covering with water. Bring to the boil, then cover and simmer gently for 1½–2 hours. Strain and leave to cool. Refrigerate overnight.

Put all the marinade ingredients into a bowl. Weigh the joint before putting into the bowl. Press down until almost all the meat is covered by the marinade. Cover and leave in a cool place overnight, turning at least once during that time.

Next day, skim the fat from the stock. Lift the meat from the marinade, place on a wire rack, and stand over a grill pan or roasting tin. Place in a preheated oven, gas mark 7 (220°C/425°F), and cook for 25 minutes per 0.5 kg (1 lb) of meat plus 25 minutes. Baste occasionally with the marinade. When the meat is tender, skim the fat from the pan juices and stir in a scant 275 ml (½ pint) stock, taking care to scrape any residue sticking to the bottom of the pan. Heat through, and serve with the joint.

PORK WITH ROSEMARY AND GARLIC

A delicious way to cook pork. The hint of garlic and rosemary complements its flavour perfectly.

Serves 4

2 cloves of garlic
3-4 sprigs of fresh rosemary
675-900 g (1½-2 lb)
 boneless loin of pork
2 tablespoon white wine
 vinegar
150 ml (¼ pint) dry white
 wine

1 heaped tablespoon
 unbleached white flour
225-275 ml (8-10 fl oz)
 chicken stock (see page
 156)
freshly ground black pepper

Push the whole, unpeeled cloves of garlic and the sprigs of rosemary into the meat. Lay the joint, on its side, in a roasting tin, and brush with wine vinegar. Roast in a preheated oven, gas mark 4 (180°C/350°F), for 1½-2 hours until tender. Transfer the meat to a serving plate. Remove one of the cloves of garlic before covering the meat with foil. Keep hot until needed.

Drain the fat from the roasting tin. Crush the garlic, and put into the tin. Pour the wine over, and scrape the bottom of the tin to loosen the pan juices. Put over a moderate heat and bring to the boil. Boil briskly until reduced by two-thirds. Remove from the heat, then stir in the flour. Gradually add most of the chicken stock, stirring well after each addition. Return to the heat, and bring to the boil, stirring frequently, until the gravy thickens. Thin down with more stock if necessary. Season to taste with black pepper. Serve with the pork.

Sunday Afternoon

It seems strange that the meal consisting of some of the 'nicest' foods should be the one to have fallen from favour. Of course, during the week few people have the time to relax and enjoy afternoon tea but I doubt whether many of us sit down to such a meal at the weekends either. My guess is that the very idea of eating afternoon tea is regarded as taboo by an increasing number of health– and weight-conscious adults. While I share their concern, I also think that it would be a pity to see the tradition disappearing altogether, particularly as it need not consist of platefuls of sweet gooey cakes and buns. What could be nicer than delicate sandwiches, wholewheat scones or a light fatless sponge decorated with fresh strawberries?

Some shops specialize in very good fancy cakes which is useful for a special occasion but most shop-bought cakes are nowhere near as good as those made at home. When I was a child, in the West Riding of Yorkshire, Thursday was baking day and we children would rush home from school eager to sample the 'misshapes'. Many of the recipes included in this section are taken from an old family cookbook where the information given is sparse to say the least, and few recipes have any method or cooking times. As most are credited to relatives and friends of the family, one can only assume that if the cook couldn't work out what to do from the list of ingredients, she asked the person in question for further instructions. No doubt the system worked well fifty years ago but it has obvious drawbacks today. I have reworked the recipes to include quantities, methods and cooking times without in any way detracting from the authentic flavours of my youth.

VICTORIAN CUCUMBER SANDWICH

This recipe is taken from a small booklet called *Michael Smith's Book of Sandwiches* (BBC 1, 1979).

cucumber	1 tablespoon thick cream
salad oil	tip of 1 teaspoon ready-made
lemon juice	English mustard
salt, pepper	1 teaspoon lemon juice
	salt, pepper
CREAMED BUTTER	
50 g (2 oz) softened butter	

The cucumber must be cut as thinly as possible – ideally using a mandoline. Very lightly salt the slices, and leave them to drain in a colander. Lightly weight with a plate for 2 hours or so, pressing from time to time to get rid of excess juices.

Dress the sliced and drained cucumber with a little oil, lemon juice and a dredge of freshly ground white pepper (no more salt).

Make up the creamed butter by blending together all the ingredients. Butter thin slices of bread, fill in the usual way, but at the last possible moment, as this sandwich can become soggy.

CREAM CHEESE AND WATERCRESS SANDWICH

Spread thin slices of bread with cream cheese, and scatter finely chopped watercress on top. Make the sandwiches in the usual way.

SALTED TOMATO SANDWICH

Put the tomatoes into a pan of boiling water, and leave for 2-3 minutes. Remove, one at a time, and peel. Chop and season with salt. Butter thin slices of bread, and fill in the usual way. Make at the last possible moment.

Sunday Afternoon

PARMA HAM ROLLS

Butter thin slices of brown bread. Lay a slice of very thinly sliced Parma ham on top, and roll up tightly. Cut the roll into pinwheels with a sharp knife. Sprinkle with mustard and cress to serve.

DRESSED EGG SANDWICH

Finely chop or mash a hard-boiled egg with a fork. Season to taste with a dribble of cold pressed sesame oil, a few drops of white wine vinegar and freshly ground black pepper. Butter thin slices of bread, and fill in the usual way.

FAT RASCALS

Popular throughout the North and West Ridings, fat rascals are thought to have originated on the moors behind Whitby where they were known as turf cakes. They are a cross between a biscuit and a scone and used to be cooked on a griddle over an open turf or peat fire. Fat rascals are very easy to make - my grandmother used to add some sugar and a handful of currants to any leftover pastry at the end of her weekly baking session. Eat them plain or buttered.

225 g (8 oz) wholewheat
  self-raising flour
50 g (2 oz) lard, diced
50 g (2 oz) butter, diced
40 g (1½ oz) sugar

50 g (2 oz) currants
25 g (1 oz) sultanas
a pinch of salt (optional)
a little water *or* beaten egg

Put the flour into a bowl, then rub in the lard and butter until the mixture resembles breadcrumbs. Add the sugar, currants, sultanas and salt, if using it. Mix to a fairly soft dough with water or beaten egg. Roll out on a floured board to about 1.25 cm (½ inch) thick, and cut into rounds. Place on an oiled tray, and bake in a preheated oven, gas mark 7 (220°C/425°F), for 15–20 minutes until nicely browned.

FEATHER SCONES

Makes 7

225 g (8 oz) wholewheat
  flour
1 teaspoon cream of tartar
½ teaspoon bicarbonate of
  soda
25 g (1 oz) butter, diced

25 g (1 oz) currants
2 tablespoons natural
  yoghurt
75 ml (3 fl oz) milk (approx)
1 small egg, beaten
1-2 tablespoons milk

Mix together the flour, cream of tartar and bicarbonate of soda in a
bowl. Rub in the butter with the fingertips until the mixture resembles
breadcrumbs. Add the currants. Stir in the yoghurt, milk and most of
the beaten egg, and mix to form a soft dough. Roll out on a lightly
floured board until about 1.75 cm (¾ inch) thick, then cut into rounds.
Place on a baking tray. Mix together the remaining beaten egg with the
milk, and use to glaze the scones. Bake in a preheated oven, gas mark
7 (220°C/425°F), for 15-20 minutes until well risen and lightly
browned.

MOTHER'S PARKIN

Parkin is supposed to improve with keeping, and it was customary a few
years ago to tell anyone who was ill, 'Don't worry, you'll soon be like
parkin', presumably implying that they would improve in a little while.
In my family, parkin was made all the year round but it only appeared
in the shops around 5th November as it was customary to hand some
round the bonfire.

100 g (4 oz) medium
  oatmeal
225 g (8 oz) wholewheat
  self-raising flour
25 g (1 oz) soft brown sugar

2 teaspoons ground ginger
100 g (4 oz) golden syrup
100 g (4 oz) black treacle
175 g (6 oz) butter
1 egg, beaten

Mix together the oatmeal, flour, sugar and ginger in a bowl. Melt the
syrup, treacle and butter in a small pan, then stir the mixture into the
dry ingredients. Add the beaten egg, and pour into a lined and greased
square tin, measuring approximately 5 cm (2 inches) deep and 17.5 cm
(7 inches) across. Bake in a preheated oven, gas mark 4 (180°C/
350°F), for 1-1¼ hours until firm to the touch.

Sunday Afternoon

APPLE CINNAMON SQUARES

Makes 9

FOR THE BASE
**175 g (6 oz) wholewheat
flour
75 g (3 oz) porridge oats
150 g (5 oz) butter, diced
3-4 tablespoons cold water**

FOR THE FILLING
**675 g (1½ lb) Cox's eating
apples, peeled, cored and
sliced
50 g (2 oz) sultanas
1 level teaspoon ground
cinnamon**

Make the base first. Put the flour and porridge oats in a bowl, and rub in the butter until the mixture resembles coarse breadcrumbs. Add 3 tablespoons of the water, and mix together lightly. Firmly press half the mixture into the base of an oiled and lined square tin measuring approximately 2.5 cm (1 inch) deep and 17.5 cm (7 inches) across. Lay the apple slices over the base. Sprinkle the sultanas and cinnamon on top.

Add 1 tablespoon cold water to the remaining base ingredients, and mix to form a pastry dough. Roll out on a lightly floured board, and use to cover the apples. Dampen the edges, and press down gently on the pastry with the palm of your hand. Bake in a preheated oven, gas mark 5 (190°C/375°F), for 35 minutes until lightly browned. Cut into squares.

Sunday Afternoon

ST WILFA CAKE

This cake originates from Ripon in North Yorkshire where there is a saying, 'an apple pie without cheese is like a kiss without a squeeze'. This recipe takes the Yorkshireman's passion one step further for the cheese is actually baked inside the pastry. Wensleydale cheese gives the best results but Cheddar or Lancashire cheese can be substituted.

FOR THE PASTRY	FOR THE FILLING
225 g (8 oz) wholewheat flour	4 tablespoons apricot jam
75 g (3 oz) butter, diced	450 g (1 lb) Bramley apples, peeled, cored and thinly sliced
2 tablespoons sunflower oil	50 g (2 oz) Wensleydale cheese, grated
8 teaspoons cold water	a little milk *or* beaten egg

To make the pastry, put the flour in a mixing bowl, and rub in the butter and oil, using the fingertips, until the mixture resembles breadcrumbs. Add the water, and mix to form a pastry dough. Roll out three-quarters of the pastry on a lightly floured board, and use to line a greased tin, measuring approximately 2.5 cm (1 inch) deep and 20 cm (8 inches) across.

Spread the apricot jam over the base of the pastry. Arange the apple slices on the top. Sprinkle with the grated cheese, and cover with the remaining pastry. Brush with milk or beaten egg, and bake in a preheated oven, gas mark 6 (200°C/400°F), for 25–30 minutes until lightly browned.

PEAR AND GINGER SHORTBREAD

175 g (6 oz) wholewheat flour	1 level teaspoon ground ginger
175 g (6 oz) butter, diced	1 large ripe pear, peeled, cored and thinly sliced
75 g (3 oz) sugar	

Put the flour in a bowl, and rub in the butter, using the fingertips, until the mixture looks like coarse breadcrumbs. Stir in the sugar and ginger. Press two-thirds firmly into the base of a lined and oiled square tin, measuring approximately 2.5 cm (1 inch) deep and 15 cm (6 inches) across. Lay the pear slices on top. Sprinkle with the rest of the shortbread mixture, and press down gently. Bake in a preheated oven, gas mark 4 (180°C/350°F), for 40–45 minutes until lightly browned. Mark into slices but leave to cool in the tin.

CURRANT TEACAKES

Makes 8

450 g (1 lb) strong flour (brown *or* white)	15 g (½ oz) fresh yeast *or* 7 g (¼ oz) dried yeast
1 tablespoon soft brown sugar	275 ml (½ pint) warm milk
	75 g (3 oz) currants
	oil as required

Sift the flour into a bowl with the sugar. Blend the fresh yeast in the warm milk or reconstitute the dried yeast as directed on the packet. Add the yeast liquid to a handful of flour in a small bowl, and leave in a warm place until frothy. Pour the yeast mixture over the remaining flour, add the currants, and mix to form a dough. Knead on a lightly floured board until smooth and elastic. Leave in a warm place to double in size.

Knead the dough again and divide into eight pieces. Shape into teacakes, and place on a oiled baking tray. Leave in a warm place until well risen. Bake in a preheated oven, gas mark 6 (200°C/400°F), for 15-20 minutes until lightly browned and hollow-sounding when tapped on the bottom. Serve warm from the oven or toasted.

RAISIN PINWHEELS

Yeasted buns not unlike Chelsea buns in appearance.

Makes 9

100 g (4 oz) strong brown flour	1 tablespoon sunflower oil
100 g (4 oz) unbleached white flour	1 egg, beaten
15 g (½ oz) fresh yeast *or* 7 g (¼ oz) dried yeast	100 g (4 oz) raisins
	15 g (½ oz) butter
125 ml (4 fl oz) warm milk	1 tablespoon concentrated apple juice
	a little milk

Mix together the brown and white flours in a bowl. Blend the fresh yeast into the warm milk or reconstitute the dried yeast as directed on the packet. Add the yeast liquid to 3 tablespoons of the measured flour in a small bowl, and leave in a warm place until frothy. Pour the yeast mixture over the rest of the flour. Add the oil and most of the beaten egg, and mix to form a dough. Knead until smooth and elastic. Leave in a warm place to double in size.

Meanwhile, put the raisins, butter and concentrated apple juice in a small pan, and heat gently until the butter has melted. Leave to cool slightly.

Knead the dough again before rolling out to form a rectangle measuring 30 × 22.5 cm (12 × 9 inches). Spread the raisins and their cooking juice over the top, and roll up like a Swiss roll. Cut into nine pieces, and place on their sides on a lightly oiled baking tray. Mix together the remaining beaten egg with a little milk, and use to glaze the pinwheels. Leave in a warm place to double in size. Bake in a preheated oven, gas mark 6 (200°C/400°F), for 25 minutes until lightly browned.

APRICOT PLAIT

A lovely golden-coloured teabread.

75 g (3 oz) dried apricots
125 ml (4 fl oz) water
100 g (4 oz) strong brown
  flour
100 g (4 oz) unbleached
  white flour

7 g (¼ oz) fresh yeast *or* 1
  teaspoon dried yeast
150 ml (¼ pint) warm milk
1 egg, beaten

Dice 25 g (1 oz) apricots, put into a small pan with the water and bring to the boil. Cover and simmer gently until they begin to soften and all the water has been absorbed.

Mix together the brown and white flours in a bowl. Blend the fresh yeast in the warm milk or reconstitute the dried yeast as directed on the packet. Add the yeast liquid to a handful of flour in a small bowl, and leave in a warm place until frothy. Stir the yeast mixture into the remaining flour. Add half the beaten egg and the cooked apricots. Thinly slice the rest of the apricots, and add these to the bowl also. Mix together well to form a dough. Knead for several minutes on a lightly floured board. Leave in a warm place to double in size.

Knead the dough again until it is no longer sticky. Roll out like a sausage until it is approximately 22.5 cm (9 inches) long. Cut into three strips, and twist to form a plait. Secure the ends, and brush with the remaining egg. Leave in a warm place until risen. Bake in a preheated oven, gas mark 6 (200°C/400°F), for 20-25 minutes until lightly browned. Tap the base of the plait with the knuckles; when it sounds hollow, the teabread is done. Cool on a wire rack. Serve sliced and buttered.

SALLY LUNN

There is some uncertainty as to how the Sally Lunn came by its name. Some say that it was baked and sold in the streets of Bath by one Sally Lunn, while others claim it to be a corruption of the French *Sol et Lune* as the top of each bun is said to resemble the shining golden sun and the pale, delicately coloured base supposedly resembles the moon.

> 200 g (7 oz) unbleached
>   white flour
> 2 level teaspoons sugar
> 2 level teaspoons dried yeast
>
> 75-125 ml (3-4 fl oz) warm
>   milk (½ boiling/½ cold)
> 1 egg, beaten
> oil as required

Put a handful of measured flour in a small bowl, add the sugar, yeast and milk, and mix together. Leave in a warm place until it becomes frothy. Add the remaining flour and beaten egg, and mix to form a dough. Knead on a lightly floured board until smooth and elastic. Return to the bowl, and keep in a warm place until it has doubled in size. Knock down and knead again for a minute or so. Shape into a ball, then flatten gently until about 2.5 cm (1 inch) thick. Tuck the edges underneath, towards the centre, so that it is shaped like a pin cushion. Place on an oiled baking tray, and brush the top with the remaining beaten egg. Put in a warm place to prove and when the dough has doubled in size again, bake in a preheated oven, gas mark 6 (200°C/ 400°F), for 20-25 minutes. Tap the base with the knuckles – when it sounds hollow, the Sally Lunn is done. Eat while still warm from the oven, sliced with butter and jam.

DATE AND WALNUT BREAD

A popular teabread. There is no need to add any sugar as the dates provide all the necessary sweetness.

225 g (8 oz) strong brown flour	1 tablespoon sunflower oil
7 g (¼ oz) fresh yeast *or* 1 teaspoon dried yeast	25 g (1 oz) chopped walnuts
150 ml (¼ pint) warm water	50 g (2 oz) dates, pitted and chopped
	½ small nutmeg, grated

Sift the flour into a bowl. Blend the fresh yeast into the warm water or reconstitute the dried yeast as directed on the packet. Add the yeast liquid to 3 tablespoons of the measured flour, and leave in a warm place until frothy. Add the oil and remaining flour and mix to form a dough. Knead on a lightly floured board until smooth and elastic. Leave in a warm place until doubled in size.

Work the walnuts, dates and nutmeg into the dough, and shape into a cob. Place on an oiled baking tray, and leave in a warm place to prove. Bake in a preheated oven, gas mark 6 (200°C/400°F), for 35–40 minutes. Tap the base with the knuckles – when it sounds hollow, the teabread is done. Cool on a wire rack. Serve sliced and buttered.

ORANGE FRUIT LOAF

Another sugar-free recipe using dried fruit to sweeten the cake. Grated orange rind adds interest and flavour.

75 g (3 oz) dates, pitted and chopped	200 g (7 oz) wholewheat self-raising flour
125 ml (4 fl oz) milk	50 g (2 oz) porridge oats
2 eggs	100 g (4 oz) sultanas
75 g (3 oz) soft butter, diced	grated rind of 1 large orange

Put the dates and milk in a small pan, and bring to the boil. Simmer for 2–3 minutes before removing from the heat. Leave to cool slightly. Tip the dates and the milk into a liquidizer or food processor, then add the eggs and butter. Blend until smooth and creamy.

Put the flour, porridge oats, sultanas and orange rind in a bowl, and mix together. Stir in the blended ingredients. Spoon the mixture into a lined and greased 900 g (2 lb) loaf tin. Make a shallow hollow in the centre, and bake in a preheated oven, gas mark 4 (180°C/350°F), for 60 minutes or until a skewer pushed into the centre comes out clean.

HONEY AND WALNUT CAKE

225 g (8 oz) wholewheat
   self-raising flour
100 g (4 oz) butter, diced
40 g (1½ oz) walnuts,
   chopped

1 egg, beaten
3 tablespoons clear honey
4 tablespoons milk

Put the flour in a bowl, and rub in the butter, using the fingertips, until the mixture resembles breadcrumbs. Add the walnuts. Blend together the egg and honey in a liquidizer or food processor and pour this over the dry ingredients. Mix well. Gradually add the milk until the mixture has a stiff consistency. Spoon into a lined and greased 17.5 cm (7 inch) cake tin. Make a slight hollow in the centre and bake in a preheated oven, gas mark 4 (180°C/350°F), for 1 hour or until a skewer pushed into the centre comes out clean.

WHISKED SPONGE

4 medium eggs
a scant 100 g (4 oz) soft
   brown sugar
50 g (2 oz) fine wholewheat
   flour
50 g (2 oz) unbleached white
   flour

100g (4 oz) low fat
   cream cheese
clear honey to taste
fresh strawberries, halved
icing sugar

Put the eggs and sugar in a small bowl, and stand in a pan of hot water. Whisk until thick and creamy – the peaks left by the whisk should still be visible half a minute or so after it has been removed. Sift half the flour into the bowl, and carefully fold into the whisked mixture with a metal spoon or a spatula. Fold in the rest of the flour and any bran left in the sieve. Spoon the mixture into two lined and greased 20 cm (8 inch) sandwich tins. Bake in a preheated oven, gas mark 5 (190°C/375°F), for 20–25 minutes until lightly browned and firm to the touch. Cool on a wire rack. Sweeten the cream cheese with honey to taste. Spread over one of the cakes. Arrange the strawberries on top and cover with the remaining cake. Dust with sieved icing sugar.

Tea

Official records indicate that tea first came to this country from Holland, but I prefer to believe the story of Lady Mary Douglas. We are told that she was sent a posy from China by her lover, but by the time it reached England, the flowers had faded. Nonetheless, like all true romantics, Lady Mary couldn't bear to part with them and placed them in a vase beside her bed. That night she awoke, hot and feverish, and took a sip of the water from the vase to quench her thirst. Much to her surprise, the water tasted exceedingly good and, after making enquiries, she discovered the flowers to be those of the tea plant.

By the mid-eighteenth century, tea had become so popular in Britain that it was fast becoming the principal drink of all classes. Its appearance in some households still gave rise to bewilderment, and some people, knowing it as tcha, took to chewing it, others made it into sandwiches while one old lady boiled her entire two pound consignment and then served the leaves as a vegetable with butter and salt.

There are four basic types of tea, each having a distinctive and easily recognizable leaf and flavour. The first, green tea, was the earliest type to come to Britain. The leaves are gathered and then withered and dried. The resultant tea is light and refreshing and is usually drunk without either milk or sugar. The leaves of the second type, known as oolong, are crushed after the initial withering which causes oxidation and a change of colour from green to brown. Again, the tea is light and fragrant and is generally served black. The third category, black tea, is the one with which we are most familiar. The oxidation process is allowed to continue until the leaf is a rich, brown colour and the flavour full. Here in Britain, we almost always drink it with milk although most other nations prefer it black. The final category includes smoked teas such as lapsong souchong. They are served without milk.

Provided that the end result pleases and refreshes the palate, there is no right or wrong way to make tea but you could do worse than take the advice offered in this English rhyme:

> Unless the pot be boiling
> And the tea-pot hot,
> A good cup of tea
> Cannot be got.

Sunday Afternoon

HOT SPICY LEMON TEA

Serves 6–8

3 lemons	575 ml (1 pint) boiling water
2 oranges	a pinch of cinnamon
575 ml (1 pint) fresh tea	sugar

Carefully cut the peel from 1 lemon and 1 orange, and place in a warm earthenware bowl. Squeeze the juice from the remaining fruit, and add to the bowl with the remaining ingredients, adding cinnamon and sugar to taste. Cover and keep warm. Leave to infuse for 5-6 minutes before straining and serving.

ICED LEMON TEA

Fill a glass one-third full with cracked ice. Add the juice of half a lemon, and fill with hot, freshly made tea. Sweeten to taste. Leave to cool. Add some more ice, a slice of lemon and a sprig of mint before serving.

Weekdays

COOKING IN ADVANCE

Cabbage Rolls

= Fish & Orange Casserole =

Stocks

Seafood Pancakes

Weekdays

I am fortunate in that I usually have time to prepare a cooked meal in the evenings but, even so, I tend to avoid dishes that require lengthy preparation. I also avoid recipes requiring expensive ingredients as we all come home tired and hungry, and prefer simple, comforting food rather than anything elaborate or over fussy. There are occasions when I am grateful for canned and packaged convenience foods but they are the exception rather than the rule for what one saves in time, one loses in quality. I much prefer to make full use of my wok and pressure cooker or, if I know that time is going to be at a premium, I occasionally prepare a dish in advance or take something out of the freezer.

When I first acquired a freezer, I felt compelled to keep it full of home-made dishes, and spent the best part of every Saturday planning and preparing sufficient food to last through the coming week. In principle, this was an excellent plan but it soon became clear that it was totally impractical. Certainly, it cut down on cooking during the week, and one was assured of eating a 'proper' meal every evening but that didn't seem sufficient recompense for having to spend the best part of one's weekends shopping and cooking. I also found myself missing the opportunity to make impulsive buys when something took my fancy at the fishmonger's, greengrocer's, butcher's or at my local market. I therefore became gradually less conscientious until, of course, a happy compromise was reached. Nowadays, I tend to use my freezer for bulk-buying, batch-baking and for storing seasonal gluts of vegetables; for serving elaborate meals with the minimum of fuss and bother, and to keep a stock of unusual and exotic ingredients at my fingertips. It generally contains a hotch-potch of foods including a selection of breads, soft fruits, chopped tomatoes, sugar-free jams, smoked fish, home-made stocks, precooked dishes and leftovers. It has become a sort of extended larder, enabling me to keep perishable foods for weeks rather than days. Of course, they would keep for longer but I find that no matter how carefully one follows the instructions about wrapping, freezing and thawing foodstuffs, their flavour and texture are adversely affected, particularly over long periods.

Home-Made Stocks

Stock cubes are no alternative to a good home-made stock. I prefer to make this when I have the necessary ingredients to hand, keeping the stock in the freezer until needed.

FISH STOCK

Makes about 850 ml (1½ pints)

450 g (1 lb) fish trimmings (leftover bones, skin, heads and tails)
850 ml (1½ pints) water
150 ml (¼ pint) dry white wine (optional)

1 small onion, sliced
1 medium carrot, sliced
10 black peppercorns
1 sprig of fresh parsley
1 sprig of fresh thyme
1 bay leaf

Remove any pieces of gut or gills from the trimmings before placing them in a large pan with the other ingredients. Cover and bring to the boil. Skim, cover again and simmer for 20–30 minutes. Strain well. Freeze for up to 6 months.

CHICKEN STOCK

Makes about 725 ml (1¼ pints)

1 chicken carcass and giblets
  or 3-4 drumsticks *or* wings
1 small onion, chopped
1 small carrot, chopped
1 stick of celery, chopped
1 bay leaf
1 sprig of fresh parsley

1 sprig of fresh thyme
1 sprig of fresh marjoram
575 ml (1 pint) water
150 ml (¼ pint) dry white
  wine (optional)
10 black peppercorns

Chop the carcass, and put into a pan with the remaining ingredients. Bring to the boil, cover and simmer for 25-30 minutes. Strain. Freeze for up to 6 months.

BEEF STOCK

Makes 1.7–1.9 litres (3–3½ pints)

1.5 kg (3 lb) beef bones,
  chopped
225 g (8 oz) shin beef
2.5 litres (4 pints) water
2 onions, chopped
2 leeks, chopped

2 carrots, chopped
1 sprig of fresh thyme
1 sprig of fresh parsley
1 bay leaf
10 black peppercorns

Put the beef bones, shin beef and water in a pan, and bring to the boil. Skim off the froth, cover and simmer for 2 hours or pressure-cook at *high* pressure for 25 minutes. Add the remaining ingredients, and cook for a further 2 hours or 25 minutes respectively. Strain, cool and remove the solidified fat. Freeze for up to 6 months.

Weekdays

CROFTERS SOUP

Serves 4

1-2 tablespoons sunflower
 oil
1 onion, chopped
2 slices of lean unsmoked
 bacon, trimmed and
 chopped
50 g (2 oz) haricot beans,
 soaked overnight and then
 drained
875 ml (1½ pints) water

1 leek, sliced
2 carrots, chopped
75 g (3 oz) white cabbage,
 shredded
2 potatoes, chopped
2 tablespoons chopped fresh
 parsley
1 teaspoon mixed dried herbs
salt, pepper

Heat the oil in a large pan or pressure cooker, and gently sauté the onion for 5-7 minutes until soft and golden. Toss in the bacon and cook for a few minutes more. In a separate pan, boil the beans briskly in the water for at least 10 minutes, then add to the pan with the bacon. Add the remaining ingredients, and bring to the boil. Cover and simmer for 1¼-1½ hours until tender or pressure-cook at *high* pressure for 15 minutes. Adjust the seasoning and consistency to taste; it may be necessary to add more water if the soup has been simmered in a pan. If necessary, freeze for up to 6 weeks or keep in a refrigerator until needed.

TUSCAN SOUP

Serves 4

100 g (4 oz) haricot beans,
 soaked overnight and then
 drained
575 ml (1 pint) water
4-5 leeks, trimmed and
 sliced

275 ml (½ pint) milk
 (approx)
1-2 tablespoons chopped
 fresh parsley
juice of 1 lemon
freshly ground black pepper

In a large pan or pressure cooker, boil the beans briskly in the water for at least 10 minutes. Add the leeks, cover and simmer for 1¼-1½ hours until the beans are tender, adding more water as and when necessary or pressure-cook at *high* pressure for 15 minutes. Pass through a vegetable mouli or blend in a liquidizer or food processor until fairly smooth.

Return to the heat, then gradually add the milk until the desired consistency is reached. Heat through. Season to taste with parsley, lemon juice and black pepper. If necessary, freeze for up to 3 months or keep in a refrigerator until needed.

CURRIED LENTIL SOUP

A lovely creamy soup tasting of the Orient.

Serves 4-6

225 g (8 oz) red lentils	**½ teaspoon ground**
2 onions, chopped	**coriander**
2 potatoes, chopped	**½ teaspon ground cumin**
2 large cloves of garlic, peeled	**1.2-1.3 litres (2¼-2½ pints)**
and crushed	**water**
2 level teaspoons medium	**1 teaspoon garam masala**
curry powder	**juice of 1-2 lemons**
½ teaspoon ground ginger	**3 tablespoons chopped fresh**
	coriander

Sort through the lentils and remove any small stones or pieces of grit. Put into a pan or pressure cooker with the onions, potatoes, garlic, curry powder, ginger, coriander, cumin and most of the water. Bring to the boil, cover and cook for 45-55 minutes or pressure-cook at *high* pressure for 10 minutes. Pass the soup through a vegetable mouli or blend in a liquidizer or food processor until smooth. Add the remaining water until the desired consistency is reached. If necessary, freeze for up to 2 months or keep in a refrigerator until needed. Before serving, heat through and stir in the garam masala. Season to taste with lemon juice. Sprinkle with the chopped coriander.

PALESTINE SOUP

At first glance, Jerusalem artichokes look like small knobbly potatoes. Their knobbliness can, in fact, be a problem and, if possible, it is best to choose ones that look easy to peel. Once peeled, the white flesh quickly discolours unless put into a bowl of cold water to which a few drops of vinegar or lemon juice have been added. It is not always necessary to peel the tubers, and they can often be scrubbed and served in their skins. Remember, however, that any cut edge needs rubbing with lemon juice or immersing in slightly acidic water if left to stand.

Although Jerusalem artichokes can be cut into thin slivers and eaten raw in salads, it is more usual to serve them hot. They make excellent purées, soufflés, soups and creamy gratin dishes, and can also be braised, boiled, roasted, sautéed and steamed.

Serves 4

1 tablespoon sunflower oil	425 ml (¾ pint) water
15 g (½ oz) butter	575 ml (1 pint) milk
1 onion, chopped	salt, pepper
2 sticks of celery, chopped	1–2 tablespoons chopped
450 g (1 lb) Jerusalem	fresh chives
artichokes	

Heat the oil and butter in a pan or pressure cooker, and gently sauté the onion and celery for 5–7 minutes until soft and golden. Peel the Jerusalem artichokes, chop them, and immediately stir into the onion mixture to prevent the flesh discolouring. Pour the water over, and simmer for 25–35 minutes or pressure-cook at *high* pressure for 6–7 minutes. Pass the soup through a vegetable mouli or blend in a liquidizer or food processor until smooth. Return to the pan, and stir in the milk. If necessary, freeze for up to 3 months or refrigerate until needed. Season to taste before serving sprinkled with chives.

CELERIAC AND KIDNEY BEAN CASSEROLE

Serves 4

175 g (6 oz) red kidney
   beans, soaked overnight
   and then drained
575 ml (1 pint) water
1–2 tablespoons sunflower
   oil
1 large onion, chopped
350 g (12 oz) celeriac
3 carrots, chopped

3 tomatoes, chopped
100 g (4 oz) flat
   mushrooms, chopped
1 level tablespoon chopped
   fresh rosemary
1 tablespoon shoyu soya
   sauce
freshly ground black pepper

In a large pan or pressure cooker, boil the beans briskly in the water for at least 10 minutes, then cover and simmer for 1¼–1½ hours until tender, adding more water if necessary, or pressure-cook at *high* pressure for 20 minutes. Drain well, reserving both the beans and their stock.

Heat the oil in a casserole-type pan, and sauté the onion for 5–7 minutes until soft and golden. Peel and chop the celeriac, one by one, stirring into the sautéed onions immediately to prevent discoloration. Add the carrots, tomatoes and mushrooms, and cook for 2–3 minutes more. Stir in the rosemary and cooked beans. Pour over sufficient bean stock to cover three-quarters of the mixture. Add the soya sauce, and season to taste with black pepper. Cover and simmer for 35–40 minutes until the vegetables are tender and the casserole is rich and flavoursome. If necessary, freeze for up to 3 months or store in a refrigerator until needed.

Weekdays

ADUKI BEAN HOTPOT

The aduki bean is small, round and reddish brown in colour. It is grown throughout the Far East where it is known as the 'King of the Beans'. Reputed to be a gift from a benevolent god to an evil world, the aduki is said to have beneficial effects upon the kidneys. Folklore aside, it is an excellent source of protein, B vitamins and iron.

Serves 4

225 g (8 oz) aduki beans, soaked overnight and then drained
575 ml (1 pint) water
1–2 tablespoons sunflower oil
1 onion, chopped
1 small head of celery, chopped
1 clove of garlic, peeled and crushed

2 tablespoons chopped fresh parsley
1–2 tablespoons chopped fresh sage
1 tablespoon tomato purée
1 level tablespoon *mugi miso*
freshly ground black pepper
1–2 tablespoons chopped fresh parsley

In a large pan or pressure cooker, boil the beans briskly in the water for at least 10 minutes, then cover and simmer for 45–55 minutes until tender, adding more water if necessary, or pressure-cook at *high* pressure for 12–15 minutes. Drain well, reserving both the beans and their stock.

Heat the oil in a casserole-type pan, and sauté the onion, celery and garlic for 8–10 minutes. Add the cooked beans, parsley, sage and tomato purée. Pour sufficient stock over to cover three-quarters of the mixture. Cover and simmer for 30 minutes until the vegetables have softened and the stock thickened. Blend the *miso* with 2-3 tablespoons of stock from the casserole. Stir into the pan, and season to taste with black pepper. If necessary, freeze for up to 3 months or keep in a refrigerator until needed. Heat through and sprinkle with parsley before serving.

BUTTER BEAN AND CIDER COBBLER

If making the dish in advance, don't add the topping until the dish is ready to be cooked.

Serves 4

FOR THE FILLING
100 g (4 oz) butter beans, soaked overnight and then drained
425 ml (¾ pint) dry cider
275 ml (½ pint) water
3 carrots, sliced
3 sticks of celery, sliced
2 leeks, sliced
1 bay leaf
2 sprigs of fresh thyme
1 sprig of fresh parsley
salt, pepper

FOR THE SAUCE
25 g (1 oz) butter
25 g (1 oz) unbleached white flour
1 level teaspoon German mustard

FOR THE TOPPING
225 g (8 oz) wholewheat self-raising flour
¼ teaspoon bicarbonate of soda
a good pinch of mixed dried herbs
50 g (2 oz) butter, diced
150 ml (¼ pint) milk

To make the filling, boil the beans briskly in the water for at least 10 minutes, then add the cider, water, vegetables and herbs. Bring to the boil, then cover and simmer for 1½ hours until tender, adding more water and cider if necessary. Or pressure-cook at *high* pressure for 20 minutes. Drain and reserve the stock. Discard the herbs. Season the bean mixture to taste.

To make the sauce, melt the butter in a small pan, stir in the flour. Cook for a minute or two until the mixture bubbles. Remove from the heat, then gradually add 350 ml (12 fl oz) reserved bean stock, stirring well after each addition. Return to the heat and bring to the boil, stirring all the time, until the sauce thickens. Stir in the mustard. Pour the sauce over the bean mixture, and mix together. Spoon into a pie dish. Freeze for up to 3 months or keep in a refrigerator for a day or so until needed.

Just before baking, make the scone topping. Put the flour, bicarbonate of soda and mixed herbs in a bowl, and mix together well. Rub in the butter and add the milk. Mix to form a dough, roll out on a floured board to a thickness of 1.25 cm (½ inch), and cut into rounds about 5 cm (2 inches) in diameter. Arrange the scones on top of the filling, and brush with a little milk. Bake in a preheated oven, gas mark 6 (200°C/400°F), for 20–25 minutes until well risen and lightly browned.

Weekdays

MEXICAN BEEF WITH BEANS

Serves 4–6

100 g (4 oz) red kidney
beans, soaked overnight
and then drained
1 bay leaf
575 ml (1 pint) water
1–2 tablespoons sunflower
oil
1 onion, chopped
1 clove of garlic, peeled and
crushed
450 g (1 lb) minced beef

175 g (6 oz) button
mushrooms, halved or
quartered
450 g (1 lb) ripe tomatoes,
chopped
1 good teaspoon chilli
powder
½ teaspoon cayenne pepper
½ teaspoon allspice
salt, pepper

In a large pan or pressure cooker, boil the beans briskly in the water for at least 10 minutes, then cover and simmer for 1¼–1½ hours until tender, adding more water if necessary, or pressure-cook at *high* pressure for 20 minutes. Drain well, reserving both the beans and their stock.

Heat the oil in a casserole-type pan, and sauté the onion and garlic for 5–6 minutes until soft and golden. Add the minced beef and fry until it begins to brown. Stir in the remaining ingredients and the cooked beans. Cover and simmer for 30–35 minutes until the meat is tender. Check the pan occasionally during the cooking to make sure it is not boiling dry; add a little of the reserved bean stock if necessary – the sauce should be thick and richly flavoured. Season to taste. If necessary, freeze for up to 3 months or store in a refrigerator until needed. Serve with brown rice.

CABBAGE ROLLS

Serves 4

100 g (4 oz) chick-peas,
  soaked overnight and then
  drained
1.1 litres (2 pints) water
225 g (8 oz) brown rice
1 savoy cabbage
1-2 tablespoons sunflower
  oil
2 onions, chopped
100 g (4 oz) sultanas
1 teaspoon chilli powder
juice ½ lemon

1-2 tablespoons chopped
  fresh parsley
freshly ground black pepper

FOR THE SAUCE
25 g (1 oz) butter
1 tablespoon sunflower oil
40 g (1½ oz) unbleached
  white flour
500 ml (18 fl oz) milk
100 g (4 oz) button
  mushrooms, sliced
freshly grated nutmeg

Put the chick-peas into a large pan or pressure cooker. Pour over 575 ml (1 pint) of the water, cover and bring to the boil. Simmer for 1½ hours until tender, adding more water as and when necessary, or pressure-cook at *high* pressure for 20 minutes. Drain well.

Put the rice in another pan with a further 575 ml (1 pint) water. Bring to the boil, cover and simmer gently, without stirring, for 35–40 minutes until the rice is dry and tender.

Meanwhile, remove the large outer leaves from the cabbage. Trim and discard any tough stalks, and cook until barely tender. Drain and leave to cool.

Heat the oil in a frying pan, and sauté the onions for 5–7 minutes until soft and golden. Put into a mixing bowl, then add the cooked beans and rice, the sultanas, chilli powder, lemon juice and parsley. Season to taste with black pepper. Place 1–2 tablespoons of the mixture on each cabbage leaf, and roll up like a Swiss roll. Arrange in the base of a lightly oiled ovenproof dish.

To make the sauce, heat the butter and oil in a pan, and stir in the flour. Cook for a minute or two until the mixture bubbles. Remove from the heat, then gradually add the milk, stirring well after each addition. Return to the heat, and bring to the boil, stirring all the time, until the sauce thickens. Add the mushrooms, and season to taste with the nutmeg. Pour the sauce over the stuffed cabbage leaves. If necessary, freeze for up to 2 months or keep in a refrigerator until needed. Before serving, bake in a preheated oven, gas mark 6 (200°C/400°F), for 25–30 minutes until heated through.

VEGETABLE CURRY WITH RAITA

If you don't much like hot spicy dishes, remember to remove the white seeds from inside the green chillies, and don't use too much curry powder. The other spices – ginger, cumin and turmeric – are added for flavour rather than hotness.

Serves 4

2–3 tablespoons groundnut oil
2 onions, sliced
2 cloves of garlic, peeled and crushed
2 green chillies, finely chopped and crushed
2.5 cm (1 inch) fresh root ginger, peeled and grated
1–2 tablespoons curry powder
1 teaspoon cumin seeds
1 teaspoon turmeric

1 medium-sized cauliflower, broken into florets
2 courgettes, sliced
2 carrots, sliced
1 green pepper, chopped
150 ml (¼ pint) water

FOR THE RAITA
¼ cucumber, diced
150 ml (¼ pint) natural yoghurt
1–2 teaspoons finely chopped fresh mint

Heat the oil in a large pan, and sauté the onions for 5-7 minutes until soft and golden. Add the garlic, chillies, ginger, curry powder, cumin seeds and turmeric, and sauté for a minute or two. Add the vegetables, then pour the water over. Cover and simmer gently for 15-20 minutes until the vegetables are tender.

To make the raita, mix together all the ingredients, and spoon into an attractive dish. Serve with the curry. Accompany the dishes with Wholewheat Chapatti (see page 167).

HAZELNUT BALLS IN TOMATO SAUCE

A delicious combination. The brown hazelnut balls in a rich tomato sauce look just like meat balls but taste much better. My two young nieces thought they were wonderful although they were under the impression that they were eating round sausages – I didn't like to disillusion them!

Serves 4

FOR THE HAZELNUT BALLS
- 1–2 tablespoons olive oil
- 1 large onion, finely chopped
- 175 g (6 oz) roasted hazelnuts, ground
- 75 g (3 oz) fresh wholewheat breadcrumbs
- 75 g (3 oz) mature Cheddar cheese, grated
- 1 tablespoon chopped fresh parsley
- ¼–½ teaspoon dried mixed herbs
- 1 large egg, beaten
- salt, pepper

FOR THE SAUCE
- 1–2 tablespoons olive oil
- 1 onion, chopped
- 1 small green pepper, chopped
- 100 g (4 oz) button mushrooms, sliced
- 550 g (1¼ lb) ripe tomatoes, chopped
- 1–2 teaspoons tomato purée
- ¼–½ teaspoon dried mixed herbs
- 2–3 tablespoons red wine *or* water
- 150–200 ml (5–7 fl oz) water
- salt, pepper

To make the hazelnut balls, heat the olive oil in a frying pan, and sauté the onion for 5-7 minutes until soft and golden. Tip from the pan into a mixing bowl, and add the remaining ingredients. Mix together well, and season to taste. Shape into about 20 small balls. If necessary, place on a baking tray and freeze for up to 3 months or keep in a refrigerator until needed.

To make the sauce, heat the remaining oil in a large pan, and sauté the onion and pepper for 4–5 minutes. Add the mushrooms, and sauté for several minutes before adding the tomatoes, tomato purée, mixed herbs and wine or an equivalent amount of water. Cover and simmer gently for 20 minutes or so until the tomatoes are very soft. Pass through a vegetable mouli or blend in a liquidizer or food processor until fairly smooth. Gradually add the 150-200 ml (5-7 fl oz) water until the consistency is sauce-like – it must not be watery. Season to taste. This sauce keeps well in both the freezer (3 months) and refrigerator.

Weekdays

To cook, pour half the sauce into a shallow ovenproof dish, and arrange the hazelnut balls on top. Cover with the remaining sauce, and bake in a preheated oven, gas mark 5 (190°C/375°F), for 25-30 minutes until the hazelnut balls are heated through and the sauce is hot and bubbling. Serve with wholewheat spaghetti.

WHOLEWHEAT CHAPATTI

Makes 10–12

250 g (9 oz) chapatti flour   **150 ml (¼ pint) warm water**
   (fine wholewheat flour)   **(approx)**
1 tablespoon sunflower oil

Put the flour in a bowl, and rub in the oil. Gradually add the water, and knead to form a soft dough. Divide the dough into 12 small balls, and roll out on a floured board until each is about 15 cm (6 inches) in diameter. Cook the chapatti, one at a time, in a hot, heavy-based frying pay – no oil is needed. Cook until each side becomes speckled brown. Stack under a clean cloth while the remaining chapatti are being cooked. Use as required.

VEGTABLE LASAGNE

A delicious vegetarian lasagne.

Serves 4-6

175 g (6 oz) red lentils
1 onion, chopped
1 large clove of garlic, peeled
  and crushed
1 stick of celery, chopped
1 red pepper, chopped
100 g (4 oz) flat
  mushrooms, chopped
450 g (1 lb) ripe tomatoes,
  chopped
1 tablespoon tomato purée
1 bay leaf
1 teaspoon dried mixed herbs
2 tablespoons chopped fresh
  parsley
275 ml (½ pint) water
150 ml (¼ pint) red wine

2-3 teaspoons shoyu soya
  sauce
freshly ground black pepper
175-225 g (6-8 oz)
  wholewheat lasagne
1 tablespoon olive oil

FOR THE SAUCE
15 g (½ oz) butter
1 tablespoon olive oil
25 g (1 oz) unbleached white
  flour
275 ml (½ pint) milk
50 g (2 oz) mature Cheddar
  cheese, grated
1 tablespoon grated
  Parmesan cheese
freshly grated nutmeg

Sort through the lentils and remove any grit or small stones. Put into a large pan or pressure cooker with the onion, garlic, celery, red pepper, mushrooms, tomatoes, tomato purée, bay leaf, dried mixed herbs, parsley, water and red wine. Bring to the boil, cover and simmer for 45-50 minutes until the lentils are soft. Add more water, a little at a time, as and when necessary. If using a pressure cooker, pressure-cook at *high* pressure for 10 minutes. If the mixture is very wet, boil briskly, with the pan uncovered, to drive off any surplus water – the lentils should be reduced to a thick purée. Season to taste with soya sauce and black pepper.

Meanwhile, fill a large pan with boiling water, add the oil and lasagne, and cook briskly for 10-12 minutes until *al dente*. Drain well.

To make the sauce, heat the butter and oil in a pan, and stir in the flour. Cook for a minute or two until the mixture bubbles. Remove from the heat, then gradually add the milk, stirring well after each addition. Return to the heat, and bring to the boil, stirring all the time, until the sauce thickens. Add most of the Cheddar cheese and all the Parmesan cheese. Season to taste with nutmeg.

Brush an ovenproof dish, one about 5 cm (2 inches) deep, with olive oil, and arrange half the cooked lasagne in the base. Spoon over half the lentil mixture. Repeat the two layers, then cover with the cheese sauce. Sprinkle the remaining grated cheese over the top. If necessary, freeze for up to 3 months or keep in a refrigerator until needed.

To bake, put into a preheated oven, gas mark 6 (200°C/400°F), for 25-30 minutes until bubbling and golden-brown. Leave aside for 5-10 minutes to firm up before serving.

Note: I like to bake and serve lasagne in four individual dishes. Not only do these look particularly attractive but there is no danger of the pasta slipping off the spoon as it is being transferred from one dish to another.

FISH AND ORANGE CASSEROLE

Serves 4

3 carrots, sliced
1-2 tablespoons olive oil
1 onion, sliced
1 stick of celery, chopped
1 clove of garlic, peeled and crushed
175 g (6 oz) button mushrooms, chopped if necessary
15 g (½ oz) unbleached white flour

275-425 ml (½-¾ pint) fish stock (see page 155)
grated rind and juice of 1 orange
550 g (1¼ lb) white fish fillets (cod, haddock, whiting), skinned, boned and chopped into bite-sized pieces
salt, pepper

Boil the carrots until tender. Drain well. Meanwhile, heat the oil in a casserole-type pan, and sauté the onion and celery for 5–7 minutes until they begin to soften. Add the garlic and mushrooms, and cook for several minutes more, stirring occasionally. Stir in the flour, followed by 275 ml (½ pint) stock. Add the grated rind and juice of 1 orange and the cooked carrots, and bring to the boil. Cover and boil briskly for several minutes before reducing the heat. Add the chopped fish to the pan, and poach for several minutes until the fish is cooked. Season to taste. Serve with brown rice and a green vegetable or salad.

SEAFOOD PANCAKES

Stuffed pancakes are often described in cookery books as a 'convenient dish' and one that is 'easy to prepare' but this isn't always the case. It really does depend on the nature of the filling and how many people you are catering for.

There is nothing complicated or elaborate about this recipe but cooking it for four or more people does take time and, whenever possible, I like to prepare everything in advance. Both the stuffing and the pancakes freeze well or can be kept in the refrigerator for a day or so. I usually stuff the pancakes just before heating them through.

Serves 4–6

FOR THE FILLING
425 ml (¾ pint) fish stock (see page 155)
450 g (1 lb) Finnan haddock
350 g (12 oz) haddock fillets, skinned and chopped into bite–sized pieces
175 g (6 oz) canned *or* frozen sweetcorn kernels
50 g (2 oz) butter
50 g (2 oz) unbleached white flour
salt, pepper

FOR THE PANCAKES
225 g (8 oz) wholewheat flour
a pinch of salt (optional)
2 eggs
575 ml (1 pint) milk
1 tablespoon oil

To make the filling, put the fish stock into a pan and bring to the boil. Place the Finnan haddock in a steamer over the boiling stock, and cook for 4-5 minutes until barely tender. Put aside and leave to cool.

Meanwhile, place the chopped haddock in the pan of boiling stock, cover and remove from the heat. Leave aside while skinning and boning the Finnan haddock. Gently break the Finnan haddock into large flakes and put into a mixing bowl. Lift the haddock from the stock, flake and put into a bowl too. Add the sweetcorn.

Melt the butter in a pan, and stir in the flour. Cook for a minute or two until the mixture bubbles. Remove from the heat, then gradually add the fish stock, stirring well after each addition. Return to the heat, and bring to the boil, stirring all the time, until the sauce thickens. Pour this over the fish and sweetcorn. Carefully mix together, and season to taste.

To make the pancakes, mix together the flour and salt (if using it) in a bowl. Make a well in the centre and add the eggs. Pour in half the milk, and gradually work into the flour. Mix well until smooth. Add the remaining milk a little at a time, stirring well after each addition. Add the oil, and beat the batter vigorously until it is creamy and the surface is covered with bubbles. If using a liquidizer or food processor, put all the ingredients into the goblet and blend until smooth. Cook the batter in a hot, lightly oiled frying pan, making approximately 10 pancakes. If the pancakes are not to be used immediately, stack, interleaved with greaseproof paper. If freezing the dish, freeze the sauce and pancakes separately. Freeze for up to 3 months.

Spread 3 tablespoons of the filling mixture over each pancake, roll up like a Swiss roll. Arrange in the base of a lightly oiled, shallow ovenproof dish. Spoon the remaining filling mixture over the top, and bake in a preheated oven, gas mark 6 (200°C/400°F), for 20-25 minutes until heated through. Serve with a green salad and bread rolls.

CHICKEN PILAU WITH RICE

A pilau is an excellent way of using up leftovers. This one is particularly colourful and, although full of flavour as it stands, will obviously taste even better if chicken stock is used instead of water.

Serves 4

2 tablespoons olive oil
2 cloves of garlic, peeled and
  crushed
2 onions, chopped
1 small green pepper,
  chopped
100 g (4 oz) button
  mushrooms, sliced
2 carrots, sliced

225 g (8 oz) long grain
  brown rice
a scant 575 ml (1 pint) water
  or chicken stock
175 g (6 oz) canned *or*
  frozen sweetcorn kernels
175 g (6 oz) boned cooked
  chicken, chopped
salt, pepper

Heat the oil in a heavy-based pan, and sauté the garlic and onions for 5–7 minutes. Add the green pepper, and cook for several minutes more. Stir in the mushrooms, carrots and rice, then pour the water over, and bring to the boil. Cover and simmer for 30–35 minutes until the rice is almost tender and dry. Add the sweetcorn and chicken, and cook for a further 5-8 minutes, stirring occasionally, until heated through. Season to taste before serving.

Weekdays

CRUSTY CHICKEN AND MUSHROOM PIE

Serves 4–6

1 oven-ready chicken,
  weighing 1 kg (2.2. lb)
1 small onion, chopped
1 carrot, chopped
1 sprig of fresh thyme
1 sprig of fresh parsley
6 black peppercorns
1.1 litres (2 pints) water
2 potatoes
50 g (2 oz) canned *or* frozen
  sweetcorn kernels
100 g (4 oz) button
  mushrooms, sliced

25 g (1 oz) butter
25 g (1 oz) wholewheat flour
salt, pepper

FOR THE PASTRY
175 g (6 oz) wholewheat
  flour
75 g (3 oz) butter, diced
6 teaspoons cold water
beaten egg *or* milk to glaze

Put the chicken in a pan with the onion, carrot, thyme, parsley and black peppercorns. Pour the water over, and bring to the boil. Cover and simmer for 45 minutes – 2 hours, depending on the type and age of the bird, until tender. Lift from the pan, drain well and leave to cool. Strain the stock into a measuring jug.

Cook the potatoes in the minimum of boiling water until just tender. Drain thoroughly. When the chicken is cool enough to handle, remove and discard the skin. Separate the meat from the bones, and chop into bite-sized pieces. Put into a mixing bowl. Dice the cooked potato, and add to the bowl along with the sweetcorn and mushrooms.

Melt the butter in a saucepan, stir in the flour, and cook gently until the mixture begins to bubble. Remove from the heat, then gradually add 350 ml (12 fl oz) chicken stock, stirring well after each addition. Return to the heat, and bring to the boil, stirring all the time, until the sauce begins to thicken. Mix together with the chicken and vegetables, and season to taste. Spoon into a pie dish.

To make the pastry, put the flour into a bowl, rub in the butter, with the fingertips, until the mixture resembles breadcrumbs. Add the water, and mix to form a pastry dough. Roll out to 0.6 cm (¼ inch) thickness, and use to cover the pie dish. Trim the edges, and brush with beaten egg or milk. If necessary, freeze for up to 3 months or store in a refrigerator until needed. Bake in a preheated oven, gas mark 6 (200°C/400°F), for 25–30 minutes until golden-brown.

CHICKEN SIESTA

A cold dish which can be prepared the day before it is needed. Serve with a selection of side salads.

Serves 4-6

1 oven-ready chicken
   weighing 900 g-1.2 kg
   (2-2½ lb)
1 sprig of fresh thyme
1 sprig of fresh parsley
1 bay leaf
10 black peppercorns
½ carrot, sliced
2 slices of onion

850 ml (1½ pints) approx
   water
225 g (8 oz) long grain
   brown rice
2 small oranges
1 red pepper, chopped
100 g (4 oz) cooked peas
salt, pepper

Put the chicken in a pan with the thyme, parsley, bay leaf, peppercorns, carrot and onion. Barely cover with the water. Bring to the boil, cover and simmer for 45 minutes – 2 hours, depending on the type and age of the bird, until tender. Lift from the pan, drain well and leave to cool. Strain the stock into a measuring jug.

Put the rice in a heavy-based pan, and pour over a scant 575 ml (1 pint) chicken stock. Add the grated rind of the oranges. Cover the pan, bring to the boil, then simmer for 35-40 minutes, without stirring, until the rice is dry and tender. Leave until cold.

When the chicken is cool enough to handle, remove and discard the skin and separate the meat from the bones. Chop the meat into bite-sized pieces, and place in a mixing bowl. Remove the white pith from the oranges, and cut into pieces. Put into a bowl with the chicken. Add the chopped red pepper, cooked peas and cold rice, and mix together. Season to taste.

HERBY LENTIL RISSOLES

Makes 8–10

225 g (8 oz) red lentils
575 ml (1 pint) water
1 onion, finely chopped
1 large carrot, grated
50 g (2 oz) porridge oats
25 g (1 oz) fresh wholewheat
  breadcrumbs

1–2 tablespoons chopped
  fresh sage
1 tablespoon chopped fresh
  rosemary
2–3 teaspoons shoyu soya
  sauce
freshly ground black pepper

Sort through the lentils and remove any small stones or pieces of grit. Put in a pan with the water, cover and simmer for 45–55 minutes until soft, adding more water as and when necessary, or pressure-cook at *high* pressure for 10 minutes. Drain if necessary.

Put the cooked lentils in a bowl, and add the remaining ingredients. Mix together well, and adjust the seasoning to taste. Shape into rissoles, then place on a baking tray. If necessary, freeze for up to 3 months or keep in a refrigerator until needed. If using them that day, firm up in a refrigerator for 30 minutes before cooking. To cook the rissoles, either shallow fry until both sides are lightly browned or bake in a preheated oven, gas mark 6 (200°C/400°F), for 20-25 minutes.

PEMBROKE RABBIT

Serves 4

2–3 tablespoons sunflower
  oil
1 oven-ready rabbit, jointed
1 large onion, chopped
1 large leek, sliced
1 tablespoon ready-made
  English mustard

1 tablespoon chopped fresh
  thyme
275 ml (½ pint) dry white
  wine
salt, pepper

Heat the oil in a casserole-type pan, add the rabbit, and brown on all sides. Remove from the pan with a slotted spoon. Add the onion and leek, and sauté for several minutes until they begin to soften. Stir in the mustard and thyme, and return the rabbit to the pan. Pour the wine over, and bring to the boil. Cover and simmer for 1 hour until the rabbit is tender, then season to taste. If necessary, freeze for up to 3 months or store in a refrigerator until needed.

GYPSY STEW

Serves 4

550 g (1¼ lb) silverside of
  beef
1-2 tablespoons olive oil
1 onion, chopped
2 sticks of celery, chopped
1 clove of garlic, peeled and
  crushed
2 carrots, sliced

175 g (6 oz) swede, chopped
100 g (4 oz) shelled garden
  peas
275 ml (½ pint) red wine
1-2 tablespoons chopped
  fresh thyme
1 bay leaf
salt, pepper

Cut the beef into slices, about 1.25 cm (½ inch) thick and then into chunks. Heat the oil in a large pan, and use to brown the meat. Add the onion, celery and garlic, and cook for 4-5 minutes more, stirring frequently. Add the remaining ingredients, and bring to the boil. Cover and simmer for 1½-2 hours until the meat is tender, or pressure-cook at *high* pressure for 30 minutes. Adjust the seasoning to taste. If necessary, freeze for up to 3 months or store in a refrigerator until needed.

Weekdays

MIDDLE EASTERN KEBABS

The kebabs are accompanied by a delicious sweet and sour sauce which, if necessary, can be made in advance and kept in either the freezer or refrigerator until needed.

Serves 4-6

FOR THE SWEET AND SOUR SAUCE
50 g (2 oz) raisins
175 ml (6 fl oz) boiling water
2 tablespoons sunflower oil
15 g (½ oz) butter
2 onions, finely chopped
2.5 cm (1 inch) fresh root ginger, peeled and grated
1 rounded teaspoon turmeric

1-2 teaspoons white wine vinegar
1 teaspoon clear honey

FOR THE KEBABS
675 g (1½ lb) boned shoulder of lamb, trimmed and cut into 2.5 cm (1 inch) cubes
2 tablespoons sunflower oil

To make the sauce, put the raisins in a small bowl and pour over the water. Leave to stand for 30 minutes to plump up. Heat the oil and butter in a frying pan, and sauté the onions until soft and golden. Add the root ginger, turmeric, wine vinegar, honey, raisins and their liquid. Bring to the boil, cover and simmer for 10–15 minutes. Pass through the fine blade of a vegetable mouli or blend in a liquidizer or food processor. Return to the pan. The mixture should be fairly thick; boil rapidly to reduce if necessary.

Thread the lamb cubes on to oiled skewers, and brush with oil. Put under a hot grill, and cook, turning occasionally, for 8-10 minutes until tender. Serve with the sweet and sour sauce and a dish of brown rice.

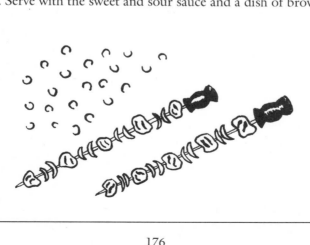

LAMB AND APPLE CASSEROLE

An unusual way of cooking chops. Although the cooking time is quite long, the dish can be left unattended in the oven, leaving you free to get on with other things.

Serves 4

1-2 tablespoons sunflower
  oil
4 lamb chops, trimmed
1 large onion, chopped
4 tomatoes, chopped
2 cloves of garlic, peeled and
  crushed

2 cooking apples, peeled,
  cored and chopped
1-2 teaspoons tomato purée
salt, pepper
225-350 ml (8-12 fl oz)
  water

Heat the oil gently in a frying pan, and fry the chops until lightly browned on both sides. Lift out and keep aside until needed. Add the onion, and sauté for 4-5 minutes until it begins to soften. Add the tomatoes, garlic and apples, and cook for several minutes more. Stir in the tomato purée, and season to taste.

Spoon half the mixture into a shallow ovenproof dish, and arrange the lamb chops on top. Cover with the remaining vegetables. Pour the water over until it is about 1.25 cm (½ inch) deep. Cover with foil or a lid, and bake in a preheated oven, gas mark 6 (200°C/400°F), for 1 hour until the chops are tender. Serve with jacket potatoes and a green vegetable.

A Seasonal Guide

Now that the novelty of eating raspberries in February and Brussels sprouts in July has worn thin, many people are once again enjoying the delights of eating something different every month of the year. Of course, there are still times when it is convenient to fall back on frozen foods, particularly those you have grown yourself, but, by and large, good cooking depends upon the use of the best and freshest ingredients.

With improved means of transport, the season for many food items has been extended, and it is now possible to eat fresh strawberries at Christmas although you have to pay dearly for the privilege and even then they are seldom as good as those grown at home. I hope that the following month-by-month guide to the availability of fresh fruit and vegetables, fish, poultry and game will help you get the best from fresh produce, and that it will serve as a guide for ingredient substitution as and where necessary.

Fresh Fruit	Home Supplies	Imported Supplies
Apples	September to May	available all year
Apricots		December to January
		June to August
Avocados		available all year
Bananas		available all year
Bilberries	July and August	
Blackberries	September and October	
Blackcurrants	July and August	
Cherries	July and August	May to September
Chestnuts		October to January
Clementines		October to January
Cranberries		October to December
Damsons	September and October	

A Seasonal Guide

Fresh Fruit	Home Supplies	Imported Supplies
Figs		August to October
Gooseberries	July and August	
Grapes		available all year
Greengages	August and September	
Grapefruit		available all year
Hazelnuts	October to January	
Kiwi fruit		available all year
Kumquats		February to April
Lemons		available all year
Limes		March to June October and November
Lychees		December to February
Mangoes		available all year
Melons		available all year
Nectarines		December to February June to September
Oranges		available all year
Peaches		December to February June to September
Pears	August to March	available all year
Pineapples		available all year
Plums	August to October	December to March June to October
Pomegranates		October to December
Raspberries	June to September	October to December
Rhubarb	December to July	
Satsumas		October to February
Strawberries	May to August	September to June
Tangerines		October to January
Uglis		November
Walnuts		August to September
Watermelon		August to September

A Seasonal Guide

Fresh Vegetables	Home Supplies	Imported Supplies
Asparagus	May to June	available all year
Aubergines	June to October	available all year
Beans, runner	July to October	available all year
Beans, French	July to September	available all year
Beans, broad	June to July	April to June
Beetroot	available all year	available all year
Broccoli (Calabrese)	May to November	November to June
Broccoli (purple sprouting)	April to May	
Brussels sprouts	September to March	
Cabbage	available all year	available all year
Carrots	available all year	available all year
Cauliflowers	available all year	available all year
Celery	available all year	January to July
Celeriac	October to March	
Chicory		available all year
Chinese Leaves	April to November	November to March May to June
Courgettes	June to October	available all year
Cucumber	March to October	available all year
Fennel	August	available all year
Garlic		available all year
Globe artichokes		available all year
Jerusalem artichokes	October to March	
Kale	November to March	
Leeks	August to May	
Lettuce	available all year	
Marrow	July to October	
Mushrooms	available all year	
Okra		available all year
Onions	available all year	available all year
Parsnips	August to April	
Peas	June to September	
Peppers		available all year
Potatoes	available all year	available all year
Spinach	April to November	November to April
Sweetcorn	August to October	January to March

A Seasonal Guide

Fresh Poultry and Game

Chicken	available all year
Duck	available all year, best August to December
Goose	September to June
Grouse	August to December
Guinea fowl	available all year, best February to April
Hare	August to March
Mallard	September to February
Partridge	October to January
Pheasant	October to January
Pigeon	available all year, best August to October
Quail	available all year
Rabbit	available all year
Snipe	August to January
Teal	September to February
Turkey	available all year
Venison	July to January
Woodcock	October to January

Fresh Fish

Bass	May to August
Sea bream	June to December
Brill	available all year, best January to April
Cod	available all year, best October to April
Coley	available all year
Conger eel	February to November
Crab	available all year
Dabs	April to January
Dover sole	available all year, best May to February
Dublin Bay prawns	available all year, best May to November

A Seasonal Guide

Grey mullet	May to March
Haddock	available all year, best November to February
Hake	available all year, best July to March
Halibut	June to April
Herring	available all year, best June to March
Lemon sole	available all year, best December to March
Lobster	available all year, best April to August
Mackerel	available all year, best January to April
Mussels	September to March
Oysters	available all year, best September to January
Plaice	available all year, best January to April
Prawns	available all year
Rainbow trout	available all year
Red mullet	May to September
Salmon	February to September
Salmon trout	April to August
Scallops	October to March
Shrimps	available all year
Skate	available all year, best October to April
Smelts	November to February
Sprats	September to March
Turbot	available all year, best April to July
Whiting	available all year
Whitebait	February to July

INDEX

Index

blanquette of rabbit, 86
blue Stilton and onion tarts, 66
boeuf à la mode, 132
braised pepper steak, 87
brandied chicken, 83
bread *see also* teabreads
  apricot plait, 147
  breakfast rolls, 105
  brioche, 111
  croissants, 109
  currant teacakes, 145
  date and walnut, 149
  eggy, with bacon, 49
  garlic, 14
  Sally Lunn, 148
breakfast rolls, 105
brioche, 111
broccoli
  and mushrooms, with soufflé omelet, 46
butter bean
  and cider cobbler, 162
  purée, with roast lamb, 133

cabbage rolls, 164
café au lait, 118
cakes *see also* teabreads
  honey and walnut, 150
  Mother's parkin, 142
  St Wilfa, 144
  whisked sponge, 150
cannellini bean
  and courgette casserole, 20
caponata with squid, 30
carbonade of beef, 89
Caribbean fruit salad, 94
carrot
  and celeriac, stir-fried, 70
cashew nut cream, 95
casseroles
  celeriac and kidney bean, 160
  chicken spiced with cumin, 125
  courgette and cannellini, 20
  fish and orange, 169
  gypsy stew, 175
  lamb and apple, 177
cauliflower
  and Gruyère soufflés, 61

and ham salad, 68
cayenne kidneys, 54
celeriac
  and carrot, stir-fried, 70
  and kidney bean casserole, 160
chapatti, wholewheat, 167
cheese dishes
  blue Stilton and onion tarts, 66
  cheese and potato pie, 48
  coeur de crème with blackcurrant purée, 98
  courgette and Gruyère omelet, 45
  cream cheese and watercress sandwich, 139
  Glamorgan sausages, 47
  individual cauliflower and Gruyère souffles, 61
  rich Cheddar soup, 11
  St Wilfa cake, 144
  sardine and cottage cheese snack, 53
  sardine rolls, 54
  speckled rice with two cheeses, 24
  tofu cheesecake, 99
  tomato macaroni cheese, 49
  yoghurt cheese, 100
cheesecake, tofu, 99
chicken
  brandied, 83
  casserole spiced with cumin, 125
  country, 123
  crusty, and mushroom pie, 172
  with herbs in foil, 29
  with mushrooms and red wine, 126
  with orange and saffron sauce, 84
  pilau with rice, 171
  siesta, 173
  stock, 156
  stuffed with apricots and almonds, 124
  and yoghurt soup, 59
chick-peas
  cabbage rolls, 164

Index

Index

Index

Index

Index

Index

spinach
  eggs Florentine, 42
  oeufs Marcel, 25
  stuffed omelet Chinese-style, 45
sponge, whisked, 150
squid, caponata with, 30
steak
  stir-fried, with lemon, 31
  braised, pepper, 87
stew, gypsy, 175
Stilton, blue, and onion tarts, 66
stir-fried dishes
  carrot and celeriac, 70
  Chinese vegetables with prawns, 26
  Dover sole, 26
  mange-tout peas, 70
  nitsuke vegetables, 16
  steak and lemon, 31
  vegetables, with tofu, 18
stocks
  beef, 156
  chicken, 156
  fish, 155
strawberries
  marinated strawberries and peaches, 96
stuffed aubergines with herbs, 79
stuffed chicken with apricots and almonds, 124
stuffed omelet Chinese-style, 45
sweet and sour liver, 37

tagliatelle with fresh herbs and pine kernels, 21
tart(s)
  asparagus and prawn, 65
  blue Stilton and onion, 66
tea, 151
  hot spicy lemon, 152
  iced lemon, 152
teabreads
  apricot plait, 147
  date and walnut, 149
  orange fruit loaf, 149
  Sally Lunn, 148

teacakes, currant, 145
tofu, 17
  cheesecake, 99
  with stir-fried vegetables, 18
tomato(es)
  au gratin, 41
  baked with chives, 73
  and courgette agrodolce, 71
  and haricot bean soup, 14
  macaroni cheese, 49
  and peppers, with French beans, 71
  salted sandwich, 139
  sauce, hazelnut balls in, 166
trout, salmon, *en papillote* with *beurre blanc* sauce, 82
Tuscan soup, 157

vegetable and egg fricassee, 41
vegetable curry with raita, 165
vegetable dishes
  baked tomatoes with chives, 73
  courgette and tomato agrodolce, 71
  fennel with saffron sauce, 72
  French beans with tomatoes and peppers, 71
  stir-fried carrot and celeriac, 70
  stir-fried mange-tout peas, 70
vegetable lasagne, 168
vegetable omelet, 46
vegetables paysanne, 15
vegetarian dishes
  aduki bean hotpot, 161
  asparagus with creamy mushroom sauce, 64
  black eye beans in beer, 18
  blue Stilton and onion tarts, 66
  butter bean and cider cobbler, 162
  cabbage rolls, 164
  celeriac and kidney bean casserole, 160
  creamy onion soup, 11
  curried lentil soup, 158
  eggs Florentine, 42
  eggs in a nest, 62